THE TWELFTH-CENTURY RENAISSANCE

MAJOR ISSUES IN HISTORY

Editor
C. WARREN HOLLISTER,
University of California, Santa Barbara

THE TWELFTH-CENTURY RENAISSANCE

EDITED BY

C. Warren Hollister

John Wiley & Sons, Inc.
New York   London   Sydney   Toronto

SERIES PREFACE

The reading program in a history survey course traditionally has consisted of a large two-volume textbook and, perhaps, a book of readings. This simple reading program requires few decisions and little imagination on the instructor's part, and tends to encourage in the student the virtue of careful memorization. Such programs are by no means things of the past, but they certainly do not represent the wave of the future.

The reading program in survey courses at many colleges and universities today is far more complex. At the risk of oversimplification, and allowing for many exceptions and overlaps, it can be divided into four categories: (1) textbook, (2) original source readings, (3) specialized historical essays and interpretive studies, and (4) historical problems.

After obtaining an overview of the course subject matter (textbook), sampling the original sources, and being exposed to selective examples of excellent modern historical writing (historical essays), the student can turn to the crucial task of weighing various possible interpretations of major historical issues. It is at this point that memory gives way to creative critical thought. The "problems approach," in other words, is the intellectual climax of a thoughtfully conceived reading program and is, indeed, the most characteristic of all approaches to historical pedagogy among the newer generation of college and university teachers.

The historical problems books currently available are many and varied. Why add to this information explosion? Because the Wiley Major Issues Series constitutes an endeavor to produce something new that will respond to pedagogical needs thus far unmet. First, it is a series of individual volumes—one per problem. Many good teachers would much prefer to select their own historical issues rather than be tied to an inflexible sequence of issues imposed by a publisher and bound together between two covers. Second, the Wiley Major Issues Series is based on the idea of approaching the significant problems of history through a deft interweaving of primary sources and secondary analysis, fused together by the skill of a scholar-editor. It is felt that the essence of a historical issue cannot be satisfactorily probed either by placing a body of undigested source materials into the hands of inexperienced students or by limiting these students to the controversial literature of modern scholars who debate the meaning of sources the student never sees. This series approaches historical problems by exposing students to both the finest historical thinking on the issue and some of the evidence on which this thinking is based. This synthetic approach should prove far more fruitful than either the raw-source approach or the exclusively second-hand approach, for it combines the advantages— and avoids the serious disadvantages—of both.

Finally, the editors of the individual volumes in the Major Issues Series have been chosen from among the ablest scholars in their fields. Rather than faceless referees, they are historians who know their issues from the inside and, in most instances, have themselves contributed significantly to the relevant scholarly literature. It has been the editorial policy of this series to permit the editor-scholars of the individual volumes the widest possible latitude both in formulating their topics and in organizing their materials. Their scholarly competence has been unquestioningly respected; they have been encouraged to approach the problems as they see fit. The titles and themes of the series volumes have been suggested in nearly every case by the scholar-editors themselves. The criteria have been (1) that the issue be of relevance to undergraduate lecture courses in history, and (2) that it be an issue which the scholar-editor knows thoroughly and in which he has done creative work. And, in general, the second criterion has been given precedence over the first. In short, the question "What are the significant historical issues today?" has been answered not by general editors or sales departments but by the scholar-teachers who are responsible for these volumes.

University of California,   *C. Warren Hollister*
Santa Barbara

CONTENTS

INTRODUCTION

In 1927 the distinguished American medievalist Charles Homer Haskins published his *Renaissance of the Twelfth Century*. He intended his title as a challenge—a calculated dissent from the stereotyped picture of an Italian Renaissance bursting forth in the fifteenth century after a thousand years of medieval darkness. "The title of this book," Haskins writes, "will appear to many to contain a flagrant contradiction. A renaissance in the twelfth century! Do not the Middle Ages, that epoch of ignorance, stagnation, and gloom, stand in the sharpest contrast to the light and progress and freedom of the Italian Renaissance which followed?" Haskins' answer to this rhetorical question is an emphatic no, yet his effort to demonstrate the vitality and creativity of twelfth-century culture was an attack against an all-but-impregnable bastion of engrained historical attitudes and habits of thought. The term "Twelfth-Century Renaissance" is familiar to every European historian today, but it has not yet made a significant impact on the historical presuppositions of the intelligent American laymen. The older view—of the millennium of darkness and the great Italian awakening—is implicit in the very terms we use in our historical periodization. Consider the value judgments that lurk in such names as "Classical Antiquity," "the medieval period" or "Middle Ages," "the Renaissance," "the Reformation," "the Enlightenment." Of these terms, "Classical," "Renaissance," "Reformation," and "Enlightenment" betoken good and admirable things. "Medieval" is clearly bad—the sort of term that one might apply to the apartheid policy or the midnight curfew. "Middle Ages" is at best a neutral term suggesting a colorless age, lacking in accomplishment and historical distinctiveness, an age of intermission between two creative eras—the "Classical" and the "Renaissance."

This terminology arises from the biases of generations long past. It evolved between the mid-fifteenth and mid-nineteenth centuries, and historians today, even though they would reject or seriously qualify the historical assumptions that evoked the terms, are disinclined to reject the terms themselves. They have done good service; historians know what they mean (in a general way, at least), and they have deep roots in the historical literature and in college catalogues. They will continue to be used, and the student of history must approach them with an open mind, stripping them of their emotional suggestiveness, and using them merely as markers for chronological epochs, regions of cultural homogeneity, and boundaries of conventional textbooks and courses. Indeed, the sensitive student ought to ask not merely, "Was the medieval period necessarily superstitious and backward?" but further, "Is there necessarily any intellectual coherence in the concept of the 'Middle Ages' as a distinct cultural epoch running from about A.D. 400 or 500 to the eve of the Italian Renaissance? What has sixth-century Europe in common with thirteenth-century Europe? Might our traditional historical eras have been divided in entirely different ways with at least equally useful results?"

Still, we are bound by convention to the traditional epochs identified by their conventional labels. A few medievalists have urged the total rejection of the term "Renaissance." A good many have attacked from another viewpoint, conceding that there was an Italian Renaissance, but insisting at the same time that it was merely one of many. Thus we now have an imposing sequence of medieval renaissances—the Northumbrian Renaissance, the Carolingian Renaissance, the Ottonian Renaissance, the Renaissance of the Twelfth Century, and so on. Besides pointing up the virtues of their various periods, these medieval "renaissances" have the further effect of cheapening the word through overuse.

If the medievalist seems excessively anxious to discover renaissances within the Middle Ages he can perhaps be forgiven. For he has long been on the defensive in his endeavor to show that a real distinction exists between the terms "Middle Ages" and "Dark Ages." Much of the Italian Renaissance scholarship over the last century has been rooted in Jacob Burckhardt's brilliant, tendentious book, *The Civilization of the Renaissance in Italy*, published in 1860. "In the Middle Ages," Burckhardt writes, "both sides of human consciousness—that which was turned within as that which was turned without—lay dreaming or half awake beneath a common veil. The veil was woven of faith, illusion, and childish prepossession, through which the world and history were seen clad in strange hues." This naive generalization, purporting to describe the varieties of human experience over a thousand-year period, raises some doubt as to who it really was who saw history clad in strange hues. No scholar today, whether a specialist in the Middle Ages or the Italian Renaissance, would defend this interpretation.

Yet the debate continues. A few medievalists, overreacting, are inclined to doubt that there was anything of interest happening in fifteenth- and sixteenth-century Italy—surely nothing that could be called a renaissance. Others—both medievalists and Italian Renaissance historians—will concede that tremendously important things were happening in twelfth-century Europe but will deny that these things can properly be subsumed under the term "renaissance." There was vitality in the Middle Ages, they would say—at least from the eleventh century onward—but there was only one Renaissance and it happened in Italy.

These arguments raise the fundamental question: What do we mean by "renaissance"? Technically the concept may well be limited to its literal meaning: rebirth. A rebirth of what? Traditionally, the answer would be, a rebirth of the forms and spirit of classical antiquity in fifteenth-century Italy. The medievalist may then point out that the Carolingian scholars of the seventh and eighth centuries demonstrated an absorbing interest in classical culture, that John of Salisbury in the twelfth century was a model classical humanist, that one cannot accuse St. Thomas Aquinas of being shackled by the typically medieval veneration for the authority of Aristotle and applaud the liberated minds of Renaissance Italy for rejecting medieval scholasticism and turning back to the Greeks. But it would then be argued, on the contrary, that although medieval scholars venerated the forms of the classical past they failed to grasp its spirit. Spirits, however, are notoriously difficult to grasp, and the argument can be expected to continue for some time to come.

The more common lay conception of "renaissance" embodies

not so much a recovery of a past as a new beginning—a period of dynamic and fruitful growth. One often encounters the popular notion that the Italian Renaissance marked the genesis of urban society, personal liberation, rationalism, and science—the birth of modern man, which is to say, the first appearance on the human scene of a group of people who had the happy and admirable quality of being rather like us. These views, imprecise, intellectually vulgar, and in certain instances ludicrously wrong, nevertheless express what is probably the most widely held nonprofessional interpretation of the word "renaissance." If the term carries such loose and contradictory meanings—ranging from birth to rebirth, from the revival of classical Latin grammar to the rise of commerce and industry—one may well conclude that "renaissance" ought to be stricken from the historical vocabulary, whether with respect to the fifteenth century, the twelfth century, or any period whatever. But as the historian R. W. Southern has observed, " 'Renaissance' is no more misleading than any other word. It achieves indeed the sort of sublime meaninglessness which is required in words of high but uncertain import."

Many books have been devoted to the problem of whether there was a renaissance in fifteenth-century Italy. This one is not. To be sure, any careful evaluation of medieval culture is bound to cast some light on the question, "How novel was the Italian Renaissance?" But the chief burden of this volume will be to examine some of the significant new things that were happening in the twelfth century.

Realizing that history cannot be cut into uniform hundred-year segments, Haskins began his "Twelfth-Century Renaissance" somewhere in the mid-eleventh century and ended it somewhere in the mid-thirteenth.[1] The approximately 200 years of the "Twelfth-Century Renaissance" constituted an era of remarkable growth in European thought, art, literature, politics, and economics. It witnessed the rise of towns and commerce, the maturation of Romanesque architecture and the invention and perfection of the Gothic style, the first sophisticated polyphonic music in man's history, the expression of constitutionalism in political theory and practice, the birth of romantic love in the modern

---

[1] Similarly, the fifteenth-century Italian Renaissance is conventionally bounded by about A.D. 1350 and 1550.

sense, an upsurge of philosophical rationalism, a rapid rise in population and food production, an important movement toward the liberation of serfs, dramatic changes in the forms and expression of Christian piety, an ardent interest in classical literature, the emergence of the first universities, and many other phenomena of the highest historical importance. Whether these changes can be properly described as a "renaissance" will be debated in the early pages of this volume. The remainder of the book will be devoted to examinations and analyses of the changes themselves. That the changes occurred is beyond dispute. Their significance, however, is a matter of disagreement and constant reinterpretation. The selections included here will suggest the limitations as well as the achievements of the "Twelfth-Century Renaissance" and will leave the reader free to develop his own evaluation.

PART ONE
The Haskins Thesis

THE STATEMENT OF THE THESIS

1 FROM   *Charles Homer Haskins*
The Renaissance of the Twelfth Century

*This excerpt is taken from Haskins' classic statement of the
"Twelfth-Century Renaissance" hypothesis, first set forth in 1927. In
reading this passage, and the following selections in Section I, these
questions should be constantly borne in mind: How does the author
define "renaissance"—as a revival of ancient classicism or as a general
cultural and economic upsurge? Is the author's definition identical to
the reader's?*

The European Middle Ages form a complex and varied as well
as a very considerable period of human history. Within their
thousand years of time they include a large variety of peoples,
institutions, and types of culture, illustrating many processes of
historical development and containing the origins of many phases
of modern civilization. Contrasts of East and West, of the North
and the Mediterranean, of old and new, sacred and profane, ideal
and actual, give life and color and movement to this period, while
its close relations alike to antiquity and to the modern world
assure it a place in the continuous history of human development.
Both continuity and change are characteristic of the Middle Ages,
as indeed of all great epochs of history.

SOURCE. Charles Homer Haskins, *The Renaissance of the Twelfth Century*, Cambridge, Mass.: Harvard University Press, 1927, pp. 3–16. Reprinted by permission of the publishers. Copyright 1927, by the President and Fellows of Harvard College; copyright 1955 by Clare Allen Haskins.

This conception runs counter to ideas widely prevalent not only among the unlearned but among many who ought to know better. To these the Middle Ages are synonymous with all that is uniform, static, and unprogressive; "mediaeval" is applied to anything outgrown, until, as Bernard Shaw reminds us, even the fashion plates of the preceding generation are pronounced "mediaeval." The barbarism of Goths and Vandals is thus spread out over the following centuries, even to that "Gothic" architecture which is one of the crowning achievements of the constructive genius of the race; the ignorance and superstition of this age are contrasted with the enlightenment of the Renaissance, in strange disregard of the alchemy and demonology which flourished throughout this succeeding period; and the phrase "Dark Ages" is extended to cover all that came between, let us say, 476 and 1453. Even those who realize that the Middle Ages are not "dark" often think of them as uniform, at least during the central period from *ca.* 800 to *ca.* 1300, distinguished by the great mediaeval institutions of feudalism, ecclesiasticism, and scholasticism, and preceded and followed by epochs of more rapid transformation. Such a view ignores the unequal development of different parts of Europe, the great economic changes within this epoch, the influx of the new learning of the East, the shifting currents in the stream of mediaeval life and thought. On the intellectual side, in particular, it neglects the mediaeval rivival of the Latin classics and of jurisprudence, the extension of knowledge by the absorption of ancient learning and by observation, and the creative work of these centuries in poetry and in art. In many ways the differences between the Europe of 800 and that of 1300 are greater than the resemblances. Similar contrasts, though on a smaller scale, can be made between the culture of the eighth and the ninth centuries, between conditions *ca.* 1100 and those *ca.* 1200, between the preceding age and the new intellectual currents of the thirteenth and fourteenth centuries.

For convenience' sake it has become common to designate certain of these movements as the Carolingian Renaissance, the Ottonian Renaissance, the Renaissance of the Twelfth Century, after the fashion of the phrase once reserved exclusively for the Italian Renaissance of the fifteenth century. Some, it is true, would give up the word renaissance altogether, as conveying false impressions of a sudden change and an original and distinct culture in the fifteenth century, and, in general, as implying that there ever can be a real revival of something past; Mr. Henry Osborn Taylor prides himself on writing two volumes on *Thought and Expression in the Sixteenth Century* without once using this forbidden term. Nevertheless, it may be doubted whether such a term is more open to misinterpretation than others, like the Quattrocento[1] or the sixteenth century, and it is so convenient and so well established that, like Austria, if it had not existed we should have to invent it. There was an Italian Renaissance, whatever we choose to call it, and nothing is gained by the process which ascribes the Homeric poems to another poet of the same name. But—this much we must grant—the great Renaissance was not so unique or so decisive as has been supposed. The contrast of culture was not nearly so sharp as it seemed to the humanists and their modern followers, while within the Middle Ages there were intellectual revivals whose influence was not lost to succeeding times, and which partook of the same character as the better known movement of the fifteenth century. To one of these this volume is devoted, the Renaissance of the Twelfth Century, which is also known as the Mediaeval Renaissance.

The renaissance of the twelfth century might conceivably be taken so broadly as to cover all the changes through which Europe passed in the hundred years or more from the late eleventh century to the taking of Constantinople by the Latins in 1204 and the contemporary events which usher in the thirteenth century, just as we speak of the Age of the Renaissance in later Italy; but such a view becomes too wide and vague for any purpose save the general history of the period. More profitably we may limit the phrase to the history of culture in this age—the complete development of Romanesque art and the rise of Gothic; the full bloom of vernacular poetry, both lyric and epic; and the new learning and new literature in Latin. The century begins with the flourishing age of the cathedral schools and closes with the earliest universities already well established at Salerno, Bologna, Paris, Montpellier, and Oxford. It starts with only the bare out-

---

[1] Fifteenth Century (1400s)

lines of the seven liberal arts and ends in possession of the Roman
and canon law, the new Aristotle, the new Euclid and Ptolemy,
and the Greek and Arabic physicians, thus making possible a new
philosophy and a new science. It sees a revival of the Latin classics,
of Latin prose, and of Latin verse, both in the ancient style of
Hildebert and the new rhymes of the Goliardi,[2] and the formation of the liturgical drama. New activity in historical writing
reflects the variety and amplitude of a richer age—biography,
memoir, court annals, the vernacular history, and the city chronicle. A library of *ca.* 1100 would have little beyond the Bible
and the Latin Fathers, with their Carolingian commentators, the
service books of the church and various lives of saints, the textbooks of Boethius and some others, bits of local history, and
perhaps certain of the Latin classics, too often covered with
dust. About 1200, or a few years later, we should expect to find,
not only more and better copies of these older works, but also
the *Corpus Juris Civilis* and the classics partially rescued from
neglect; the canonical collections of Gratian and the recent
Popes; the theology of Anselm and Peter Lombard and the other
early scholastics; the writings of St. Bernard and other monastic
leaders (a good quarter of the two hundred and seventeen volumes of the Latin *Patrologia* belong to this period); a mass of
new history, poetry, and correspondence; the philosophy, mathematics, and astronomy unknown to the earlier mediaeval tradition and recovered from the Greeks and Arabs in the course of
the twelfth century. We should now have the great feudal epics
of France and the best of the Provençal lyrics, as well as the
earliest works in Middle High German. Romanesque art would
have reached and passed its prime, and the new Gothic style
would be firmly established at Paris, Chartres, and lesser centres
in the Ile de France.

A survey of the whole Western culture of the twelfth century
would take us far afield, and in many directions the preliminary
studies are still lacking. The limits of the present volume, and
of its author's knowledge, compel us to leave aside the architecture and sculpture of the age, as well as its vernacular literature,

2 Wandering scholars who composed satirical and irreverent Latin verse.
This footnote and all subsequent ones, unless otherwise indicated, are the
editor's.

and concentrate our attention upon the Latin writings of the period and what of its life and thought they reveal. Art and literature are never wholly distinct, and Latin and vernacular cannot, of course, be sharply separated, for they run on lines which are often parallel and often cross or converge, and we are learning that it is quite impossible to maintain the watertight compartments which were once thought to separate the writings of the learned and the unlearned. The interpenetration of these two literatures must constantly be kept in mind. Nevertheless, the two are capable of separate discussion, and, since far more attention has been given to the vernacular, justification is not hard to find for a treatment of the more specifically Latin Renaissance.

Chronological limits are not easy to set. Centuries are at best but arbitrary conveniences which must not be permitted to clog or distort our historical thinking: history cannot remain history if sawed off into even lengths of hundreds of years. The most that can be said is that the later eleventh century shows many signs of new life, political, economic, religious, intellectual, for which, like the revival of Roman law and the new interest in the classics, specific dates can rarely be assigned, and that, if we were to choose the First Crusade in 1096 as a convenient turning-point, it must be with a full realization that this particular event has in itself no decisive importance in intellectual history, and that the real change began some fifty years earlier. At the latter end the period is even less sharply defined. Once requickened, intellectual life did not slacken or abruptly change its character. The fourteenth century grows out of the thirteenth as the thirteenth grows out of the twelfth, so that there is no real break between the mediaeval renaissance and the Quattrocento. Dante, an undergraduate once declared, "stands with one foot in the Middle Ages while with the other he salutes the rising star of the Renaissance"! If the signature of the thirteenth century is easy to recognize in the literature, art, and thought of *ca.* 1250, as contrasted with the more fluid and formative epoch which precedes, no sharp line of demarcation separates the two. We can only say that, about the turn of the century, the fall of the Greek empire, the reception of the new Aristotle, the triumph of logic over letters, and the decline of the creative period in Latin and

French poetry, mark a transition which we cannot overlook, while two generations later the new science and philosophy have been reduced to order by Albertus Magnus and Thomas Aquinas. By 1200 the mediaeval renaissance is well advanced, by 1250 its work is largely done. In a phrase like "the renaissance of the twelfth century," the word "century" must be used very loosely so as to cover not only the twelfth century proper but the years which immediately precede and follow, yet with sufficient emphasis on the central period to indicate the outstanding characteristics of its civilization. For the movement as a whole we must really go back fifty years or more and forward almost as far.

Furthermore, the various phases of the movement do not exactly synchronize, just as in the later Renaissance there is not complete parallelism between the revival of classical learning, the outburst of Italian art, and the discoveries of Columbus and Copernicus. Certainly the revival of the Latin classics begins in the eleventh century, if indeed it may not be regarded as a continuous advance since Carolingian times, while the force of the new humanism is largely spent before the twelfth century is over. The new science, on the other hand, does not start before the second quarter of the twelfth century, and once begun it goes on into the thirteenth century in unbroken continuity, at least until the absorption of Greek and Arabic learning is completed. The philosophical revival which starts in the twelfth century has its culmination in the thirteenth. Here, as throughout all history, no single date possesses equal importance in all lines of development.

Unlike the Carolingian Renaissance, the revival of the twelfth century was not the product of a court or a dynasty; and, unlike the Italian Renaissance, it owed its beginning to no single country. If Italy had its part, as regards Roman and canon law and the translations from the Greek, it was not the decisive part, save in the field of law. France, on the whole, was more important, with its monks and philosophers, its cathedral schools culminating in the new University of Paris, its Goliardi and vernacular poets, its central place in the new Gothic art. England and Germany are noteworthy, though in the spread of culture from France and Italy rather than in its origination; indeed, the period in Germany is in some respects one of decline as we approach the thirteenth century, while England moves forward in the closest relation with France, as regards both Latin and vernacular culture. Spain's part was to serve as the chief link with the learning of the Mohammedan world; the very names of the translators who worked there illustrate the European character of the new search for learning: John of Seville, Hugh of Santalla, Plato of Tivoli, Gerard of Cremona, Hermann of Carinthia, Rudolf of Bruges, Robert of Chester, and the rest. Christian Spain was merely a transmitter to the North.

Such names, for the most part only names to us, suggest that the twelfth century lacks the wealth and variety of striking personalities in which the Italian Renaissance abounds. It has no such mass of memoirs and correspondence, its outstanding individuals are relatively few. Nor can it claim the artistic interest of portraiture. Its art is rich and distinctive both in sculpture and architecture, but it is an art of types, not of individuals. It has left us no portraits of scholars or men of letters, very few even of rulers or prelates. It has not even given us likenesses of its horses, such as adorn the palace of the Gonzaga dukes at Mantua.

Of the antecedent conditions which produced this intellectual revival, it is not easy to speak with much definiteness. The eleventh century is in many ways obscure, while the tenth is obscurer still, and the origins of intellectual movements are not easy to trace under the most favorable circumstances. One very obvious fact in the later eleventh century is the rapid development of trade and commerce, particularly in Italy, and the consequent quickening of urban life in the same region. One is tempted to draw a parallel with the economic and urban antecedents which recent writers have emphasized as explaining the Italian Renaissance of the Quattrocento; but the renaissance of the twelfth century was not specifically Italian, indeed it was in some respects most marked beyond the Alps, where economic revival had scarcely begun, so that the movement cannot be explained solely in the terms so dear to economic determinism. There was also a certain amount of political advance, as seen in the Norman lands of England and Sicily, in Catalonia, and in the process of feudal consolidation in France, an advance which

promoted a certain degree of peace and the travel and communication which go on best in a peaceful society. All these
influences counted in the Mediterranean and also in the intercourse between the Mediterranean and the Northern lands, while
the more prosperous feudal and royal courts were . . . centres
which favored literature both Latin and vernacular. The church,
of course, shared in the growing prosperity, so that among both
regular and secular clergy there was more to spend for travel
and for the buying and copying of manuscripts, and thus greater
physical opportunity for learning and study. The growth of the
papal monarchy drew clerks and laymen in ever increasing numbers along the road to Rome, also frequented, like the other
great routes of pilgrimage, by a crowd of religious wayfarers
for whom many of the *chansons de gestes*[3] were produced. Moreover, the closer definition of the ecclesiastical system was reflected in the pamphlet literature of the investiture controversy,
in the canonistic writings which followed, and in general in a
larger and better organized body of written records of every
sort.

While a general quickening of the spirit naturally accompanied
the more active life of this age, a more direct connection with
the intellectual movement can, in some instances, be shown. Thus
the revival of the Roman law in Italy toward 1100 was closely
associated with the growth of economic and social conditions to
which this superior jurisprudence was applicable. The formation
of the pilgrimage romances went with the growing number of
pilgrims who took the road to Rome and Compostela.[4] The translations of scientific and philosophical works from the Arabic
depended upon the Christian reconquest of Northern Spain,
which reached Toledo in 1085 and Saragossa in 1118, thus opening the learning of the Saracens to the Christian scholars from
the North who turned eagerly to the Peninsula. The translations
from the Greek were facilitated by the Norman conquest of
Sicily and Southern Italy, and by the commercial and diplomatic
relations maintained with Constantinople by the city republics

---

[3] "Songs of great deeds." The *Song of Roland* is a typical example.
[4] The shrine of Santiago de Compostela in Spain was, together with Rome
and Jerusalem, one of the three great pilgrimage centers of the Middle Ages.

of the North. The geographical position of Salerno undoubtedly assisted its rise to dominance in mediaeval medicine. History grew more voluminous and varied as action increased in variety and interest; histories of the Crusades required Crusaders even before historians!

Time was when the Crusades themselves would have served as an ample explanation of this, as of every other change of the twelfth and thirteenth centuries. Did not "these costly and perilous expeditions" strengthen (or weaken!) monarchy, exalt the Papacy, undermine feudalism, create the towns, set free the human spirit, and in general usher in a new age? Does not Gibbon, for example, declare that the poverty of the crusading barons "extorted from their pride those charters of freedom which unlocked the fetters of the slave, secured the farm of the peasant and the shop of the artificer, and gradually restored a substance and a soul to the most numerous and useful part of the community"? Unfortunately for all such easy guesses and facile rhetoric, historians now distinguish between the Crusades and the age of the Crusades, and point out that they were only one phase, and that not the most important, of the life of a vigorous epoch. They brought East and West into closer contact, stimulated trade, transportation, and the use of money, and helped to accelerate many tendencies already at work; but their specifically intellectual consequences are less tangible and probably less significant. Gibbon rightly saw that "the ardor of studious curiosity was awakened in Europe by different causes," if not entirely by "more recent events"; and a recent writer has pointed out that "a man may travel much and yet see little," so that "St. Louis, as Joinville shows him to us, or Joinville himself, was not intellectually changed by his crusading." [5] In any case the Crusades fail us as a cause of the Latin Renaissance, for it began well before the First Crusade, and the two movements scarcely touch.

When we have exhausted all such explanations, good or bad, there remains a final residuum which does not yield to these methods of proximate analysis. Anselm, Abaelard, Irnerius, Turold (or whoever be the author of the *Song of Roland*), Adelard

[5] E. J. Passant, in *Cambridge Medieval History*, v. 331 (Haskins' footnote).

of Bath at one end of the century, Frederick II, Francis of Assisi, and the great schoolmen at the other, cannot be accounted for by reckonings of time and milieu, still less by an inheritance which (save perhaps for Frederick II) we can no longer trace. Between such manifestations of individual genius and the vague generalization that so active an age in men's affairs was likely to be active also in the things of the mind, there is still room for further inquiry as our knowledge grows. Such inquiry needs particularly to be pushed back into the eleventh century, that obscure period of origins which holds the secret of the new movement, well before those events of crusade and conquest which fail as explanations chiefly because they come too late. Meanwhile we may simplify the problem in some degree by remembering that we have to deal with an intensification of intellectual life rather than with a new creation, and that the continuity between the ninth and the twelfth centuries was never wholly broken. While it is true in general that "each succeeding mediaeval century, besides inheriting what had become known in the time immediately preceding it, endeavored to reach back to the remote past for further treasure," the twelfth century reached out more widely and recovered more.

DISSENT AND QUALIFICATION

2 FROM *Erwin Panofsky*
Renaissance and Renascences in Western Art

*The distinguished art historian Erwin Panofsky discusses and con-
trasts here the Carolingian Renaissance, the Twelfth-Century Renaissance, and the Italian Renaissance. The first centered on the Frankish
court of Charlemagne and his son Louis the Pious, in the eighth and
ninth centuries. In analyzing the Twelfth-Century Renaissance,
Panofsky distinguishes between two distinct movements: (1) the so-
called "proto-Renaissance," centering in northern Italy and southern
France—regions where Roman remains abounded—and expressing itself in Romanesque architecture and sculpture; and (2) a movement
of "proto-humanism," arising in northern France and England, more
self-consciously classical because of its geographical separation from
the ancient centers of Roman civilization, expressing itself in classical
scholarship and literature. Both the twelfth-century "proto-Renaissance" and twelfth-century "proto-humanism," Panofsky states, declined and disappeared in the thirteenth century with the rise of the
Gothic style and the shift of attention from classical letters to philo-
sophic rationalism. In general, Panofsky's analysis constitutes a
thoughtful, qualified rebuttal of the Haskins thesis. For reasons of
space, much of Panofsky's detailed analysis and a number of illustra-
tive art reproductions have been deleted. The interested student
would be well advised to read in full the book from which this excerpt is taken.*

SOURCE. Erwin Panofsky, *Renaissance and Renascences in Western Art*,
second edition, Stockholm: Almqvist and Wiksell, 1965, pp. 36, 38–39, 42–43,
82–86, 100–103, and 106–113. Copyright 1960 by Almqvist and Wiksell. Reprinted by permission of the author and the publisher.

From the fourteenth through the sixteenth century . . . and from one end of Europe to the other, the men of the Renaissance were convinced that the period in which they lived was a "new age" as sharply different from the mediaeval past as the mediaeval past had been from classical antiquity and marked by a concerted effort to revive the culture of the latter. The only question is whether they were right or wrong. . . .

. . . The very self-awareness of the Renaissance would have to be accepted as an objective and distinctive "innovation" even if it could be shown to have been a kind of self-deception. Such, however, is not the case. It must be admitted that the Renaissance, like a rebellious youth revolting against his parents and looking for support to his grandparents, was apt to deny, or to forget, what it did owe, after all, to its progenitor, the Middle Ages. To assess the amount of this indebtedness is the bounden duty of the historian. But after this assessment has been made, the balance, I believe, is still in favor of the defendant; in fact, some of his unacknowledged debts have turned out to be compensated for by unclaimed assets.

It is perhaps no accident that the factuality of the Italian Renaissance has been most vigorously questioned by those who are not obliged to take a professional interest in the aesthetic aspects of civilization—historians of economic and social developments, political and religious situations and, most particularly, natural science—but only exceptionally by students of literature, and hardly ever by historians of art.

The student of literature will find it difficult to deny that Petrarch, in addition to "restoring to the waters of Mount Helicon their pristine clarity," set up new standards of verbal expression and aesthetic sensibility as such. . . . It is a difference in kind when Petrarch, in determining the sequence of elements in a sonnet, could base his decision on considerations of euphony ("I thought of changing the order of the first four stanzas so that the first quatrain and the first terzina would have come second and vice versa, but gave it up because then the fuller sound would have been in the middle and the hollower at the beginning and the end") while Dante had analyzed the content of every sonnet or canzone by "parts" and "parts of parts" ac-

cording to the precepts of scholastic logic. It is quite true that
a few bishops and professors climbed mountains long before
Petrarch's "epoch-making" ascent of Mont Ventoux; but it is
equally true that he was the first to describe his experience in
a manner which, depending on whether you like him or not, may
be praised as full of sentiment or condemned as sentimental.

Similarly, the art historian . . . will have to accept the basic
facts that a first radical break with the mediaeval principles of
representing the visible world by means of line and color was
made in Italy at the turn of the thirteenth century; that a second
fundamental change, starting in architecture and sculpture rather
than painting and involving an intense preoccupation with classical antiquity, set in at the beginning of the fifteenth; and that a
third, climactic phase of the entire development, finally syn-
chronizing the three arts and temporarily eliminating the dichot-
omy between the naturalistic and the classicistic points of view,
began at the threshold of the sixteenth. . . .

The first of our preliminary questions may thus be answered in
the affirmative: there was a Renaissance "which started in Italy
in the first half of the fourteenth century, extended its classicizing tendencies to the visual arts in the fifteenth, and subsequently
left its imprint upon all cultural activities in the rest of Europe."
There remains the second: can qualitative or structural—as opposed to merely quantitative—differences be shown to distinguish
not only this Renaissance from earlier, apparently analogous,
revivals but also these earlier revivals from each other? And, if
so, is it still justifiable to define the latter as "mediaeval" phenomena?

We all agree that the radical alienation from the Antique that
characterizes the high and late phases of what we call the Gothic
style—an alienation evident . . . in every work of art produced north
of the Alps after about the middle of the thirteenth and before
the end of the fifteenth century and, as will be seen, a prerequi-
site for the crystallization of the *buona maniera moderna* even
in Italy—did not result from a steady decline of classical traditions. Rather it may be said to mark the lowest point on an
undulating curve of alternate estrangements and *rapprochements;*
and it is precisely because Byzantine art had never reached such

a nadir that it would not have achieved a full-scale Renaissance even if Constantinople had not been conquered by the Turks in 1453.

The first of these *rapprochements* . . . is known as the Carolingian *renovatio*.[1] . . .

Carolingian art . . . revived and re-employed scores of "images" in which classical form was happily united with classical content and often not only endowed these images with an expressive power entirely foreign to their prototypes but also, as I have phrased it, "permitted them to escape from their original context without abandoning their original nature." The iconographical significance of these images, however, remained unchanged. The transformation of, say, Orpheus into Christ, Polyhymnia into the Virgin Mary, classical poets into Evangelists, Victories into angels, had been a *fait accompli* in Early Christian art, and the Carolingians do not seem to have taken further steps in this direction. The classical images were either left *in situ*, so to speak, as is the case wherever illuminated manuscripts were copied in their entirety; or they were made to serve a different purpose (and thereby tended to be transposed into a different medium). . . .

Nowhere in Carolingian art . . . do we seem to encounter an effort to infuse into a given classical image a meaning other than that with which it had been invested from the outset: an Atlas or a river-god in the Utrecht Psalter may immeasurably surpass his model in animation and expressiveness, but he remains an Atlas or a river-god; we are confronted with quotations or paraphrases, however skillful and spirited, rather than with reinterpretations. Conversely—and this is even more important— nowhere in Carolingian art do we seem to encounter an effort to devise a formula that might translate a given classical (or otherwise secular) text into a new picture: where illustrations of such texts were available, they were copied and recopied without cease; where none were available, none were invented.

In both these respects the simultaneous rise of proto-Renaissance and proto-humanism[2] effected an essential change. . . .

[1] Renewal.
[2] The two components, according to Panofsky, of the Twelfth-Century Renaissance. See the editor's introduction to this excerpt.

The sculptors of the eleventh, twelfth and thirteenth centuries repeated on a new level what the Early Christian artists had so extensively done but what their Carolingian heirs had so conspicuously refrained from doing: they subjected classical originals to an *interpretatio Christiana*,[3] the term *Christiana* here meant to include, in addition to that which can be found in Scripture or in hagiology,[4] all kinds of concepts that come under the heading of Christian philosophy. Antoninus Pius . . . was transformed into St. Peter, Hercules into Fortitude, Phaedra into the Virgin Mary, Dionysus into Simeon; *Venus Pudica* could be changed into Eve, and *Terra* into Luxury.

At the same time, however, classical concepts as well as classical characters (real or imaginary) and classical narratives (historical or mythical) came to be picturalized in a manner entirely independent from classical representational sources. The Four Elements and the Seven Liberal Arts, Socrates and Plato, Aristotle and Seneca, Pythagoras and Euclid, Homer and Alexander the Great, Pyramus and Thisbe, Narcissus and Europa, the heroes of the Trojan war and all the classical gods were depicted either according to the conventions familiar to the artist from the life and art of his day or on the basis of verbal descriptions—which, incidentally, for the most part were furnished by secondary rather than primary sources; in contrast to the great number of postclassical compilations, commentaries and paraphrases provided with illustrations by mediaeval book illuminators, only three scantily illustrated Virgils and hardly any illustrated Ovid have come down to us from the Middle Ages.

All these illustrations bear witness to a curious and, in my opinion, fundamentally important phenomenon which may be described as the "principle of disjunction": wherever in the high and later Middle Ages a work of art borrows its form from a classical model, this form is almost invariably invested with a non-classical, normally Christian, significance; wherever in the high and later Middle Ages a work of art borrows its theme from classical poetry, legend, history or mythology, this theme is quite invariably presented in a non-classical, normally contemporary, form.

[3] Christian interpretation.
[4] The literature relating to the lives of the saints.

To some extent this "principle of disjunction" would seem to
operate even in literature. Short poems as convincingly "antique"
as Matthew of Vendôme's *Hermaphroditus* are not too frequent,
and epics classical in language and meter as well as in content
are in a minority as compared to treatments of classical myth
and fable in very mediaeval Latin or one of the vernacular lan-
guages. . . .

In the representational arts of the high and later Middle Ages,
however, the "principle of disjunction" applies almost without
exception, or only with such exceptions as can be accounted for
by special circumstances; from which results the paradox that—
quite apart from the now familiar generic difference between
sculpture and painting—an intentionally classicizing style is found
in the ecclesiastical rather than in the secular sphere, in the decoration of churches, cloisters and liturgical objects rather than in
the representations of mythological or other classical subjects
which adorned the walls of sumptuous private dwellings and
enliven the interesting "Hansa Bowls," not to mention the minia-
tures in secular manuscripts.

In the pictures accompanying Remigius of Auxerre's *Commentary on Martianus Capella*—which, though composed in the ninth
century, did not begin to be illustrated until about 1100—Jupiter
is represented in the guise of a ruler enthroned, and the raven
which, according to the text, belongs to him as his sacred bird
of augury is surrounded by a neat little halo because the illustra-
tor involuntarily assimilated the image of a ruler enthroned and
accompanied by a sacred bird to that of Pope Gregory visited
by the dove of the Holy Spirit. Apollo—he, too, faithfully represented according to the indications of the text—rides on what
looks like a peasant's cart and carries in his hands a kind of nose-
gay from which emerge the figures of the Three Graces as little
busts. The Greek and Trojan heroes and heroines, referred to as
"barons" and "damsels" in the vernacular accounts of the Trojan
cycle, invariably move in a mediaeval environment, act according to mediaeval customs and are clad in mediaeval armor or dress.
Achilles and Patroclus as well as Medea and Jason and Dido
and Aeneas are shown engaged in playing chess. Laocoön, the
"priest," appears tonsured. Thisbe converses with Pyramus
through a wall separating two abbreviated Gothic buildings and
waits for him on a Gothic tomb slab whose inscription ("Hic

situs est Ninus rex"[5]) is preceded by the then indispensable cross. Pygmalion is represented as a practitioner of *la haute couture*, putting the finishing touches to an elaborate mediaeval dress which he has provided for his beautiful statue. . . .

From the eleventh and twelfth centuries, then, mediaeval art made classical antiquity assimilable by way of decomposition, as it were. It was for the Italian Renaissance to reintegrate the separated elements. Rendering unto Caesar the things which are Caesar's, Renaissance art not only put an end to the paradoxical mediaeval practice of restricting classical form to non-classical subject matter but also broke the monopoly of architecture and sculpture with regard to classicizing stylization. . . . And we need only to look at Michelangelo's *Bacchus* and *Leda*, Raphael's Farnesina frescoes, Giorgione's *Venus*, Correggio's *Danae*, or Titian's mythological pictures to become aware of the fact that in the Italian High Renaissance the visual language of classical art had regained the status of an idiom in which new poems could be written—just as, conversely, the emotional content of classical mythology, legend and history could come to life in the dramas (non-existent as such throughout the Middle Ages), epics and, finally, operas devoted to such subjects as Orpheus and Eurydice, Cephalus and Procris, Venus and Adonis, Lucrece and Tarquin, Caesar and Brutus, Antony and Cleopatra.

When thirteenth-century Mantua resolved to honor its secular patron saint, Virgil, by public monuments, the poet was portrayed, like the representatives of the liberal arts on the Portail Royal at Chartres, as a mediaeval scholar or canonist seated before his desk and busily engaged in writing; and it was this image which took the place of the Christ in Majesty when Mantua decided in 1257 to pattern its coins after the Venetian *grosso*. But when in 1499, at the very threshold of the High Renaissance, Mantegna was asked to design a statue of Virgil—meant to replace another monument said to have been on the Piazza d'Erbe and to have been destroyed by Carlo Malatesta almost exactly one century before—he conceived of Virgil as a truly classical figure, proudly erect, clad in a toga and addressing the beholder with the timeless dignity of a Demosthenes or Sophocles.

This reintegration was, however, preceded—and, in my opinion,

---

[5] "Here King Ninus was buried."

predicated upon—a general and radical reaction against the classicizing tendencies that had prevailed in proto-Renaissance art
and proto-humanistic writing. In Italy the seals and coins post-
dating the *Augustales* of Frederick II[6] and what I have called the
"deceptively antique" cameos produced in the thirteenth century
became progressively less rather than more classical in style.
Nicolo Pisano's own son, Giovanni, while keenly responding to
the expressive value of classical art and even daring to employ a
Venus pudica type for the representation of Prudence in his Pisa
pulpit, repudiated the formal classicism of his father and started
what may be called a Gothic counterrevolution which, in spite
of certain fluctuations, was to win out in the second half of the
fourteenth century; and it was from this Trecento[7] Gothic rather
than from the lingering tradition of Nicolo's classicism that the
buona maniera moderna of Jacopo della Quercia, Ghiberti and
Donatello arose.

In France the classicizing style of Reims was . . . submerged
by an altogether different current exemplified by the *Mary Annunciate* right next to the famous *Visitation* and nearly contemporary with it; and next to this *Mary Annunciate* there can be
seen the figure of the Angel Gabriel, produced only about ten
or fifteen years later, in which classical equilibrium has been
abandoned in favor of what is known as the "Gothic sway."
How High Gothic ornament was purged of classical motifs, how
the acanthus gave way to ivy, oak leaves and water cress and
how the Ionic and Corinthian capitals, retained or even revived
in Romanesque architecture, were banned is known to all. . . .

Analogous observations can be made in other fields, especially
in that of literature. In the course of the thirteenth century the
content of classical philosophy, historiography and poetry, though
enormously augmented and popularized, came to be . . . completely absorbed in the high-mediaeval system of thought, imagination and expression . . . and the linguistic form of Latin writing
completely emancipated itself from classical models. Unlike Bernard of Chartres, John of Salisbury, Bernardus Silvestris, or
Alanus de Insulis,[8] the great scholastics of the thirteenth and
fourteenth centuries no longer modelled their style upon the prose

---

[6] Died in 1250.   [7] Fourteenth century.
[8] Scholars during the Twelfth-Century Renaissance.

of Cicero or Suetonius, much less upon the verse of Virgil, Horace, Lucan, or Statius. It was, in fact, the very ascendancy of scholasticism, pervading and molding all phases of cultural life, which more than any other single factor contributed to the extinction of "proto-humanistic" aspirations: scholastic thinking demanded and produced a new language—new not only with respect to syntax but also to vocabulary—which could do justice to the principle of *manifestatio* (or, as I once ventured to express it, "clarification for clarification's sake") but would have horrified the classics—as it was to exasperate Petrarch, Lorenzo Valla, Erasmus, and Rabelais. . . .

In short, before the Italian High Renaissance performed its task of reintegration, that undulating curve which, as I said, may serve to describe the fluctuations of classicizing tendencies in postclassical art had reached the zero mark in all genres as well as in all countries. The later phases of the Middle Ages had not only failed to unify what the Antique itself had left to its heirs as a duality—visible monuments on the one hand, texts on the other—but even dissolved those representational traditions which the Carolingian *renovatio* had managed to revive and to transmit as a unity.

The "principle of disjunction" thus cannot be accounted for by the accidents of transmission alone. It would seem to express a fundamental tendency or idiosyncrasy of the high-mediaeval mind which we shall re-encounter on several later occasions: an irresistible urge to "compartmentalize" such psychological experiences and cultural activities as were to coalesce or merge in the Renaissance; and, conversely, a basic inability to make what we would call "historical" distinctions. And this leads us back to the question which was posed at the beginning of this chapter: can the three phenomena which we have been considering—the Italian *rinascita*,[9] the Carolingian *renovatio* and the twin movement known as proto-Renaissance and proto-humanism—be shown to differ from each other not only in scale but also in structure? And, if so, is it still possible to distinguish, within this triad of phenomena, between the Renaissance with a capital "R" and the two mediaeval revivals which I propose to call "renascences"? This question, too, deserves, I think, an affirmative answer; for,

[9] I.e., rebirth.

to put it briefly, the two mediaeval renascences were limited and transitory; the Renaissance was total and permanent.

The Carolingian *renovatio* pervaded the whole of the empire and left no sphere of civilization untouched; but it was limited in that it reclaimed lost territory rather than attempting to conquer new lands. It did not transcend a monastic and administrative *Herrenschicht*[10] directly or indirectly connected with the crown; its artistic activities did not include major sculpture in stone; the models selected for imitation were as a rule productions of the minor arts and normally did not antedate the fourth and fifth centuries A.D.; and the classical values—artistic as well as literary —were salvaged but not "reactivated" (as we have seen, no effort was made either to reinterpret classical images or to illustrate classical texts *de novo*).

The classical revival of the eleventh and twelfth centuries, on the other hand, penetrated many strata of society. In art it sought and achieved monumentality, selecting models of greater antiquity than those normally chosen by the Carolingian masters, and emancipated classical images from what I have called the stage of quotation and paraphrase (it did precisely what the Carolingian *renovatio* had failed to do in that new meanings were infused into classical images and a new visual form was given to classical themes). But it was limited in several other respects: it represented only a special current within the larger stream of contemporary civilization (whereas Carolingian civilization as a whole was coextensive with the *renovatio* movement) and was restricted to particular regions; there was, according to these regions, a basic difference between a recreative and a literary or antiquarian response to the Antique; the proto-Renaissance in the arts was virtually restricted to architecture and sculpture as opposed to painting; and in art as well as literature classical form came to be divorced from classical content. Both these mediaeval renascences, finally, were transitory in that they were followed by a relative or—in the Northern countries—absolute estrangement from the aesthetic traditions, in art as well as literature, of the classical past.

How things were changed by the real, Italian Renaissance can be illustrated by a small but significant incident. The Carolingian *Aratea* manuscript which includes, among so many other classi-

[10] Aristocratic social stratum.

cizing pictures, the Pompeian-looking Gemini . . . had been left
untouched for about four hundred years. Then a well-meaning
scribe saw fit to repeat the entire text in the script of the thirteenth century (see illustration) because he evidently thought
that the Carolingian "Rustic Capital" would stump his contemporaries, as well as future generations. But the twentieth-century
reader finds Carolingian script easier to decipher than Gothic,
and this ironic fact tells the whole story.

Our own script and letter press derive from the Italian Renaissance types patterned, in deliberate opposition to the Gothic,
upon Carolingian and twelfth-century models which in turn
had been evolved on a classical basis. Gothic script, one might say,
symbolizes the transitoriness of the mediaeval renascences; our
modern letter press, whether "Roman" or "italic," testifies to the
enduring quality of the Italian Renaissance. Thereafter, the classical element in our civilization could be opposed (though it should
not be forgotten that opposition is only another form of depen-
dence); but it could not entirely disappear again. In the Middle
Ages there was in relation to the Antique a cyclical succession of
assimilative and non-assimilative stages. Since the Renaissance the
Antique has been constantly with us, whether we like it or not.
It lives in our mathematics and natural sciences. It has built our
theatres and cinemas as opposed to the mediaeval mystery stage.
It haunts the speech of our cab driver—not to mention the motor
mechanic or radio expert—as opposed to that of the mediaeval
peasant. And it is firmly entrenched behind the thin but thus far
unbroken glass walls of history, philology and archaeology.
    The formation and, ultimately, formalization of these three

disciplines—foreign to the Middle Ages in spite of all the Carolingian and twelfth-century "humanists"—evince a fundamental
difference between the mediaeval and the modern attitude towards
classical antiquity, a difference which makes us understand the
essential strength and the essential weakness of both. In the Italian
Renaissance the classical past began to be looked upon from a
fixed distance, quite comparable to the "distance between the eye
and the object" in that most characteristic invention of this very
Renaissance, focused perspective. As in focused perspective, this
distance prohibited direct contact—owing to the interposition of
an ideal "projection plane"—but permitted a total and rationalized
view. Such a distance is absent from both mediaeval renascences.
"The Middle Ages," as has recently been said, "never knew that
they were mediaeval. The men of the twelfth century had none
of that awareness of a Cimmerian night from which—as Rabelais
wrote his friend Tiraqueau in 1532—humanity had emerged."

The Carolingian revival had been started because it was felt that
a great many things needed overhauling: the administrative system, the liturgy, the language, and the arts. When this was realized, the leading spirits turned to antiquity, both pagan and
Christian (and even with a strong initial emphasis on the latter),
much as a man whose motor car has broken down might fall back
on an automobile inherited from his grandfather which, when
reconditioned . . . , will still give excellent service and may even
prove more comfortable than the newer model ever was. In other
words, the Carolingians approached the Antique with a feeling
of legitimate heirs who had neglected or even forgotten their
property for a time and now claimed it for precisely those uses
for which it had been intended.

In contrast to this untroubled sense of legitimacy, the high-
mediaeval attitude toward the Antique is characterized by an
ambivalence somewhat analogous to that which marks the high-
mediaeval position toward Judaism. Throughout the Christian
era the Old Testament has been recognized as the foundation of
the New, and in Carolingian art the relation between the Church
and the Synagogue still tended to be interpreted in a spirit of
hopeful tolerance stressing that which perfect and imperfect
revelation have in common instead of that which separates them:
an initial in the Drogo Sacramentary produced at Metz between

826 and 855 depicts the Church and the Synagogue in a state of peaceful coexistence rather than as enemies. From the turn of the first millennium, however, . . . a feeling of hostility towards the living adherents of the Old Dispensation began to outweigh the respect for the dead patriarchs and prophets. And from the twelfth century, when this hostility resulted in discriminatory practices and physical persecution, the Synagogue came to be depicted blindfolded instead of merely turning away from the light and was occasionally shown in the act of killing an animal (although a man as tolerant as Abbot Suger of St.-Denis could still prefer to represent her, in one of his "anagogical" windows, in the role of precursor rather than foe, "unveiled" by God and thus belatedly endowed with sight, where her more fortunate sister receives a crown). In the high-mediaeval period, then, we can observe an unresolved tension between the enduring sense of obligation towards the prophetic message of the Old Law and the growing repugnance towards its bloody ritual and its contemporary manifestations. The Apostles could be shown seated or standing on the shoulders of the prophets much as Bernard of Chartres compared his generation's relation to the classics to that of dwarves "who have alighted on the shoulders of giants" and "see more numerous and distant things not by virtue of their own keen vision or their own stature but because they are raised aloft by the giants' magnitude"; but in the same iconographical context (in the "*Fürstenportal*" of Bamberg Cathedral) the Synagogue could be portrayed as a stubborn, benighted enemy of the Church, her statue surmounting the figure of a Jew whose eyes are being put out by a devil.

Similarly there was, on the one hand, a sense of unbroken continuity with classical antiquity that linked the "Holy Roman Empire of the Middle Ages" to Caesar and Augustus, mediaeval music to Pythagoras, mediaeval philosophy to Plato and Aristotle, mediaeval grammar to Donatus—and, on the other, a consciousness of the insurmountable gap that separated the Christian present from the pagan past (so that in the case of Aristotle's writings a sharp distinction was made, or at least attempted, between what was admissible and what should be condemned). The classical world was not approached historically but pragmatically, as something far-off yet, in a sense, still alive and, therefore, at once potentially useful and potentially dangerous. It is significant that the classical philosophers and poets were frequently represented in the same Oriental costumes as the Jewish prophets, and that the thirteenth century spoke of the Romans, their monuments and their gods as *sarrazin* or *sarazinais*,[11] employing the same word for the pagans of old and the infidels of its own age.

For want of a "perspective distance" classical civilization could not be viewed as a coherent cultural system within which all things belonged together. Even the twelfth century, to quote a competent and unbiased observer, "never considered the whole of classical antiquity, . . . it looked upon it as a storehouse of ideas and forms, appropriating therefrom such items as seemed to fit in with the thought and actions of the immediate present." Every phenomenon of the classical past, instead of being seen in context with other phenomena of the classical past, thus had to have one point of contact, and one of divergence, with the mediaeval present: it had to satisfy both the sense of continuity and the feeling of opposition. . . .

Now we can see why the union of classical form and classical content, even if retained in the images revived in Carolingian times, was bound to break apart, and why this process of "disjunction" was so much more radical in the arts—where the very fact that they provided a visual rather than intellectual experience entailed the danger of *curiositas*[12] or even idolatry—than in literature. To the high-mediaeval mind Jason and Medea (even though she tended to perform her tricks of rejuvenation with the aid of the "water of Paradise") were acceptable as long as they were depicted as Gothic aristocrats playing chess in a Gothic chamber. Classical gods and goddesses were acceptable as long as they lent their beautiful presence to Christian saints, to Eve or to the Virgin Mary. But a Thisbe clad in classical costume and waiting for Pyramus by a classical mausoleum would have been an archaeological reconstruction incompatible with the sense of continuity; and an image of Mars or Venus classical in form as well as significance was either, as we have seen, an "idol" or talisman or, conversely, served to personify a vice. We can understand that the same Magister Gregorius who studied and measured the

[11] Saracens, Muslims.
[12] Vain curiosity.

Roman buildings with the detachment of an antiquarian was filled with wonder and uneasiness by the "magical attraction" of that too beautiful *Venus;* that Fulcoius of Beauvais (died sometime after 1083) was able to describe a head of Mars discovered by a plowman only in terms of a violent conflict between admiration and terror . . . ; that there sprang up, as a sinister accompaniment to proto-humanism, those truly terrifying tales . . . about the young man who had put his ring on the finger of a Venus statue and thereby fell prey to the devil; and that, as late as in the second half of the fourteenth century, the Sienese believed the public erection of such a statue, recently excavated and much admired as a "work of Lysippus," to be responsible for their defeat at the hands of the Florentines (they took it down, dismembered it, and surreptitiously buried the fragments in enemy territory).

The "distance" created by the Renaissance deprived antiquity of its realness. The classical world ceased to be both a possession and a menace. It became instead the object of a passionate nostalgia which found its symbolic expression in the re-emergence—after fifteen centuries—of that enchanting vision, Arcady. Both mediaeval renascences, regardless of the differences between the Carolingian *renovatio* and the "revival of the twelfth century," were free from this nostalgia. Antiquity, like the old automobile in our homely simile, was still around, so to speak. The Renaissance came to realize that Pan was dead—that the world of ancient Greece and Rome . . . was lost like Milton's Paradise and capable of being regained only in the spirit. The classical past was looked upon, for the first time, as a totality cut off from the present; and, therefore, as an ideal to be longed for instead of a reality to be both utilized and feared.

The Middle Ages had left antiquity unburied and alternately galvanized and exorcised its corpse. The Renaissance stood weeping at its grave and tried to resurrect its soul. And in one fatally auspicious moment it succeeded. This is why the mediaeval concept of the Antique was so concrete and at the same time so incomplete and distorted; whereas the modern one, gradually developed during the last three or four hundred years, is comprehensive and consistent but, if I may say so, abstract. And this is why the mediaeval renascences were transitory; whereas the Renaissance was permanent. Resurrected souls are intangible but have the advantage of immortality and omnipresence. Therefore

the role of classical antiquity after the Renaissance is somewhat
elusive but, on the other hand, pervasive—and changeable only
with a change in our civilization as such.

3   *Eva Matthews Sanford*
The Twelfth Century—Renaissance or Proto-Renaissance?

*Professor Sanford's article was presented at a symposium on the
"Twelfth-Century Renaissance" at the 1950 annual meeting of the
Mediaeval Academy of America. After a careful review of twelfth-
century culture, Professor Sanford concludes that the term "Twelfth-
Century Renaissance," although useful as a teaching device, may well
be misleading in its tendency to obscure the vital differences between
twelfth-century France and fifteenth-century Italy. Strictly speaking,
she observes, the twelfth-century revival was neither a renaissance
nor a proto-renaissance—neither a rival to the later Renaissance nor
an anticipation of it, but a unique achievement.*

    There are two phases of our problem: what do we mean by a
renaissance, and does the twelfth century conform to this definition sufficiently to justify giving it the name? Since the term was
first applied to the humanism of the Italian *Quattrocento* and to
the appropriation of the antique in combination with direct observation of man and nature in its art, its original connotations were
in the fields of classical scholarship and of literature and art. The
humanists' reaction against their own concept of mediaevalism,
as a period of dull stagnation dominated by blind acceptance of
authority, and limited by indifference to the material world gave
rise to the idea of "rebirth" or *renaissance*, and to Michelet's
classic phrase, "the rediscovery of the world and of man." Few
scholars would now insist on the literal meaning of the word
"Renaissance," with its suggestion of a preceding state of coma,

SOURCE. Eva Matthews Sanford, "The Twelfth Century—Renaissance or
Proto-Renaissance?" in *Speculum*, Vol. XXVI, 1951, pp. 635–641. Copyright
1951 by *Speculum*. Reprinted by permission of *Speculum*.

if not of actual death, though it is difficult to wean undergraduates from this prejudiced view of the Middle Ages. If we substitute the criterion of intensified interest and vitality for rebirth
and rediscovery, we still have to reckon with the Renaissance
factors of individualism, secularism, skeptical criticism of traditional authority, and the creation of new standards and techniques
in scholarship, literature and the arts, based in part on the inter-
working of classical and contemporary factors. We have also to
consider the conspicuous influence on humanistic scholars and
artists, and on Renaissance thought in general, of the "notion of
belonging to a new time" and of the historical definition of the
Renaissance as the transition from the mediaeval to the modern
world.

In a recent paper Professor Wallace Ferguson has discussed our
need of a new synthesis of the Renaissance as "an age of moral,
religious, intellectual and aesthetic crisis, closely interrelated with
acute economic, political and social crisis."[1] He considers the
revival of antiquity as a great, but secondary, causative force in
this age. He notes decisive changes in all countries of western
Europe from the beginning of the fourteenth century, and therefore proposes that the Renaissance, as the transition from mediaeval
to modern culture, should be dated from about 1300 to 1600. This
proposal embodies a most comprehensive view of the Renaissance.
It accents the principle of crisis as a determinant, an extension of
the "new age" emphasis, and it reminds us of a chronological
problem. If we consider the twelfth century, according to Professor Haskins' chronology, as extending to about 1250, when
"the signature of the thirteenth century" became clearly recog-
nizable in literature, art, and thought, the period between a
Renaissance of the twelfth century and the inauguration of the
major Renaissance would be only fifty years long. This may lead
us to a fruitful application of the obvious differences between
the organic phenomena of the two periods, the one representing
the height of mediaeval culture, and the other a decidedly transitional phase, but both contributing directly in their different ways
to the emergence of the modern world.

As far as literature and art are concerned, Erwin Panofsky, in

<hr>

[1] Wallace K. Ferguson has since set forth his views in his comprehensive
book, *Europe in Transition, 1300–1520* (Boston, 1962).

his brilliant essay on "Renaissance and Renascences," proposed
the terms "proto-humanism" and "proto-Renaissance" for the
twelfth century, on the ground that (1) the appropriation of the
antique in this period, however notable in its immediate results,
was subjective and fragmentary, as contrasted with the focussed
perspective and comprehensive interests of the true Renaissance,
and (2) it was limited both by the strong sense of continuity with
antiquity and by Christian antagonism to pagan culture. He held
that the elements taken over from antiquity were so fully assimilated into the mediaeval patterns that they did not inspire further
progress, whereas the Italian Renaissance, though academic, was
permanent, because of the changes it created in the minds of men.
I find the specific illustrations by which he supports this thesis
more convincing in art than in literature. But he brings out an
essential difference between the two periods in their attitude
toward the classical models that both used so much in their various
ways. Writers and artists of the twelfth century did not recognize a cultural break between antiquity and their own time,
whereas those of the fifteenth century not only recognized but
emphasized it. The distinction between the twelfth century and
the later Renaissance in regard to direct stimulus provided for
further development, however, does not hold good in all the fields
that interest historians.

Professor McIlwain has demonstrated the fallacy of contrasting
the political theories and institutions of the twelfth century with
those of the Renaissance in this respect. In "Mediaeval Institutions
in the Modern World"[2] he wrote: "In the field of political institutions and ideas, I venture to think that what Professor Haskins
has termed 'the Renaissance of the Twelfth Century' marks a
more fundamental change than the later developments to which
we usually attach the word 'Renaissance'; that the constitutionalism of the modern world owes as much, if not even more, to the
twelfth and thirteenth centuries than to any later period of comparable length until the seventeenth." He cited especially the
mediaeval limitations of governmental authority by private rights,
the development of parliamentary institutions, and the gradual
assimilation of Roman constitutionalism. The slow process of

[2] Excerpts from Professor McIlwain's article are presented later in this
volume. See Part Two, Selection 5.

assimilation of Roman law was speeded up in twelfth-century Italy by the rivalries of empire, papacy, and north Italian communes, which in this period developed the autonomous institutions that contributed so much to their leadership in fifteenth century culture. The University of Bologna and the work of the great glossators show that in the field of Roman law the twelfth and thirteenth centuries left no opportunity for fundamental "discovery" but only for continued study and application of foundations already well and truly laid.

In the field of the natural sciences, we are increasingly aware that the basis for the phenomenal progress of the sixteenth and seventeenth centuries was established before the Renaissance, and that the translations of Greek and Arabic scientific works in the twelfth and thirteenth centuries provided the initial stimulus for such significant research in scientific theory and techniques as that carried on at Padua from about 1300. It is now generally recognized that Roger Bacon, as his own words testify, was not the first mediaeval scholar to set a high value on experimental science, and to formulate sound criteria for it. The net results of mediaeval science, in comparison with the achievements of the sixteenth century, are small indeed, yet the period of incubation began here rather than in the fifteenth century. In the latter period, although many humanists tended to scorn the natural sciences in favor of classical learning (as some have been known to do even in later times), the careful re-examination of mediaeval scientific works together with those of the Greeks and Romans, and the increasing interchange of ideas and techniques between scholars, artists, and craftsmen, prepared the way more fully for the dynamic scientific achievements of the sixteenth century. It would seem that in the scientific as well as in the political field the twelfth century exerted a sufficiently direct influence on later developments to make its definition as a "proto-Renaissance" untenable.

Unqualified insistence on a twelfth-century Renaissance, however, involves the risk of emphasizing the Renaissance characteristics of the period at the expense of its essentially mediaeval qualities. In many respects, like all periods of dynamic activity, it was an age of transition, but the factors of change, significant though they were, still operated to extend and enrich the traditional pat-

tern of a unified Christian culture, with its closely knit communities and personal ties, rather than to destroy them. There
were many crises in the twelfth century, but there was not, it
seems to me, the over-all motivation in terms of crisis that Professor Ferguson attributes to the later Renaissance. For all the
new phases of economic, political, social, aesthetic and intellectual
life in the twelfth century, I have not found in it that prevalent
consciousness of a new age, or the determination of ideas by the
sense of newness, that is so conspicuous in the fifteenth century.

The conviction of continuity with the ancient world is one
controlling factor here. We see it in the "Christian synthesis" of
Hebrew, Greek, Hellenistic, and Roman with Christian history,
and in the historical pattern of the four empires, ending with the
Roman, which was expected to endure till the end of the created
world. Mediaeval historians, even those who fully recognized that
the imperial power in the west had been transferred from Roman
to Frankish and German rulers, often echoed the old statement,
"The last age is the Roman, in which we now live." They did not
look back to the ideas and achievements of antiquity for fresh
inspiration from a distant source, but as a direct inheritance and
a native possession. This conviction of the unity of history made
them unconscious of anachronism and blocked off many approaches to historical criticism, but it also saved the ancient world
from the aspect of unreality that it has had for many students in
later ages. With the great increase in historical writing in the
twelfth century, the theme of *renovatio* appears, as it does also
in the political theories of the imperial partisans. Peter of Blois'
famous defence of the study of ancient history may serve to illustrate this "Renaissance" attitude, which appears frequently in the
works of the chief twelfth-century writers, but, as in this case,
within the framework of the mediaeval pattern of world history:
"However dogs may bark at me, and pigs grunt, I shall always
imitate the writings of the ancients: these shall be my study, nor,
while my strength lasts, shall the sun find me idle. We are like
dwarfs on the shoulders of giants, by whose grace we see farther
than they. Our study of the works of the ancients enables us to
give fresh life to their finer ideas, and rescue them from time's
oblivion and man's neglect." Here is no blind reverence for
ancient authority, but a dignified, though not unmodest assump-

tion that a twelfth-century scholar could and should see farther than the giants of the past. Here, also, is one of many possible answers to the common charge that mediaeval scholars in general feared and distrusted the influence of pagan ideas. The strictures of Bernard of Clairvaux and other ascetic Christians represent a significant but by no means a universal mediaeval attitude. They were often occasioned by the genuine devotion to classical literature displayed by contemporary humanists. Not only the intimate knowledge that twelfth-century writers exhibit of the works of Vergil, Ovid, Horace, and other Latin authors, but the frequent occurrence, even in theological works, of pagan *exempla virtutis* and the wide range of mediaeval quotations from classical authors, show that the classics were commonly read and used for their own value, and not merely to assail pagan corruption or to despoil the Egyptians. The extensive use of classical citations, chiefly for ethical purposes, in Petrus Cantor's *Abbreviated Word,* is one striking example of this. Another significant clue to mediaeval attitudes toward the classics is afforded by marked passages in manuscripts of the authors most read, which indicate the sentiments that the scribe, or some mediaeval reader, found particularly valuable. In the case of Juvenal, for example, one of the pagan writers classified as an *auctor ethicus,* the passages marked in many manuscripts that I have examined show clearly that he was read as a source of ethical precepts, and not merely, as some modern critics state, for evidence of pagan vice.

To those Renaissance historians who broke away from the mediaeval scheme of history, antiquity was an age long past, separated by a thousand years from their own time, and hence studied more objectively, for its possible contributions to their new and rapidly changing world. In the twelfth century, the sense of continuity with the past is conspicuous in the leading cultural centers of northern France, England, the Rhineland and the upper Danube, where the Latin language and literature were not native to the same degree that they were in southern France and Italy. Though Latin was no longer a mother tongue, even in the latter areas, it was in many respects a living language, flexibly handled by educated men, without the artificial restrictions on style and vocabulary that extreme Ciceronians later imposed on it. The hymns and lyric and narrative poems of the

twelfth and thirteenth centuries testify that poets found in Latin
a natural medium for the expression of their ideas and emotions.
The occurrence of both Latin and vernacular versions of the same
themes, and the evidences of cross-fertilization between Latin and
vernacular literature, deserve serious consideration in this connection. Greek literature, however, remained unknown, aside
from the arid and prosaic Latin epitomes of Homer, and such
works as had been earlier incorporated in the Latin tradition by
the great translators of the Roman period, or by the popular
versions of Aesop's fables and the romance of Apollonius of Tyre,
for example. The names of Greek authors were known from
histories of literature; the scholars who diligently sought out and
translated Aristotle's books on logic and natural science might pre-
sumably have recovered literary texts also, if they had wished,
but they left this important phase of the appropriation of the
antique for a later time.

Secularism, individualism, and criticism of established authority
are much stressed as distinguishing characteristics of the Renaissance. How far should our appraisal of the twelfth century be
influenced by the ecclesiastical character of its culture as contrasted with later secularism? Professor Boyce has wisely pointed
out that the terms "secular" and "ecclesiastical" are not mutually
exclusive in the Middle Ages. When education was provided
chiefly by monastic and cathedral schools, and private tutors were
usually monks or priests, when there were few non-clerical careers
for intellectual men, and students, however worldly, could claim
benefit of clergy, when all society, except for the small minority
of Jews and avowed heretics, was united in one Christian fellow-
ship, there could be no clear line of demarcation between the
religious and the secular except that drawn by extremists. Not all
priests and bishops, monks and friars were insulated from the
world by an ecclesiastical ivory tower. Those whose undue worldliness aroused the righteous indignation of contemporary reformers were sometimes, though not always, among the intellectual
leaders of their day, and some very secular works were dedicated
to ecclesiastical patrons. The learning and literature of the courts
of Henry II, Eleanor of Aquitaine, and the Norman rulers of
Sicily remind us that patronage was not entirely clerical, though
there were fewer wealthy lay patrons—as, indeed, there were

fewer wealthy men—than in the fifteenth century. Professor Thompson and others have taught us that not all the laity were illiterate, the twelfth century saw a marked increase in the reading public, and the desire of the new readers for edification and entertainment from books met with a notable response on the part of both Latin and vernacular writers. Honorius Augustodunensis, a priest and monk who chose the extremely unworldly life of an "inclusus," shows in his varied works a lively appreciation of the variety and beauties of the natural world, and a keen understanding of the material problems of the congregations for whom he composed his sermons. His writings deal not only with theological and ethical questions, but with secular history, geography, political theory, and the liberal arts. He considered this life a pilgrimage, but he made every effort to help the pilgrim live a well-rounded life during the journey of his soul to God, though he himself had narrowly restricted his own physical activities. He defined man as "a rational soul, clothed with a body," and he provided appropriate nourishment for all three elements.

The most notable buildings that afforded opportunity for the development of architecture and the decorative arts were churches, but in their decoration secular motifs were blithely introduced with apparent unconsciousness of incongruity. Though the traditional symbolism of many of these motifs is well established, the naturalism and freshness with which they are often presented makes them no less convincing evidence that details of the physical world were recognized as belonging in the religious context. As the church was the unifying factor in society, its interests embraced many secular elements which later ages associate with the body politic and social rather than with the communion of saints. Obviously, however, the ecclesiastical side of the scales was more heavily weighted than the secular, whereas the next few generations were to change the balance. Here there is a fundamental difference between twelfth-century and Renaissance culture, though the contrast is relative rather than absolute.

The question of individualism is also a relative one. We no longer identify outstanding individuals in the Middle Ages as forerunners of the Renaissance, but recognize Abelard, for example, as a natural product of his time, albeit an exceptional one.

In what age would Abelard not have been exceptional? The
personal tone of much lyric and satirical poetry is pertinent
here. Anonymity was not always due to the Christian subordination of individual claims to creative talent in favor of the Creator.
Sometimes, as in Honorius' case, it was expressly attributed to
fear of malicious opponents, and sometimes, as in the case of the
most popular treatise on education, the Pseudo-Boethius, *De
disciplina scholarium*, to the desire to gain a wider public by
fathering one's book on a noted ancient authority. Again there
is a marked difference in proportion between the two periods;
individualism is by no means exceptional in the twelfth century,
but it runs rampant in the fifteenth.

Outspoken criticism of traditional authority was not unknown
in the twelfth century, when the range of ecclesiastical questions
open to dispute was somewhat wider than it was on the eve of
the Reformation. The risk of a trial for heresy was not always a
deterrent to scholars convinced of their own sound judgment.
Skepticism and the spirit of objective inquiry did not always
provoke condemnation, and Abelard's critical method survived
numerous attacks before his works were incorporated in the
curriculum of the University of Paris. His rational thesis, "By
doubting we are led to inquire, and by inquiry we perceive the
truth," represents the constructive theological approach of the
period better than the attacks it provoked from the more intellectually inert of his contemporaries. Bishop Otto of Freising
stated the case of the imperial party against the Donations of
Constantine in a brief and matter of fact fashion without the
elaborate display of learning that was to make Lorenzo Valla's
treatise on the same subject a landmark of the critical spirit of
the Renaissance. While he left the case open, as a problem not
within the province of his *Chronicle* to decide, his presentation
leaves no doubt as to his own point of view. Honorius openly
attacked the performance for unworthy motives of such "good
works" as pilgrimages and crusades, without any inhibitions
about criticizing activities sponsored by the church.

For the Age of Faith assumed the exercise of reason, within
the bounds of its clearly defined and finite world, which still
provided ample range for speculative and critical thought. In
his memorable Harvard Tercentenary lecture on Mediaeval Uni-

versalism, Etienne Gilson pointed out the intellectual obligations imposed by the mediaeval conviction of universal truth as valid for all men at all times and places. In the twelfth century a unified society with a common meaning for all its members still transcended local differences, its culture was still non-national and non-racial, though there was an increasing consciousness of local and national distinctions. Changes were being wrought by the expansion of commerce and industry with their new contacts, implements and techniques, and their new types of communities and opportunities. Many political and social adjustments were required by these changes and by the concomitant increase in population and production. In their later stages these changes were to create a new world and in so doing, break down the unity of the old, but they had not as yet destroyed the equilibrium.

As we look back at the twelfth century, it is difficult to remember that feudal and agrarian institutions were still actively developing, with more conscious definition of their functions and principles than before, and were still being furthered rather than weakened by the expanding horizons of the age.

To sum up: the designation of the twelfth century as a proto-Renaissance seems both misleading and inadequate. But if we describe it, without considerable qualifications, as a Renaissance period, do we not risk underestimating and even distorting its real character? Can we use this term without implying more identity than the twelfth century really had with the later Renaissance, with its atmosphere of crisis and its consciousness of a new age, in which the secular motivation of political, social, economic and intellectual life replaced the universalism that still directed and inspired the thought and action of the twelfth century? I must confess that I have found the idea of a twelfth-century Renaissance very useful in teaching undergraduates mediaeval history, and I had not really questioned its validity before I wrote this paper. Now I am not so sure. If the men of the Renaissance had not put mediaevalists on the defensive by insistence on their rescue of the world and man from mediaeval ignorance and oblivion, should we feel the need of defining the earlier period as a renaissance? Should we not rather be satisfied to let the twelfth century stand on its own merits as a dynamic period of mediaeval culture, which made fruitful contributions to the development of modern man and the modern world without forfeiting its own essentially mediaeval character?

4   FROM   *Herbert J. Muller*
The Uses of the Past

Professor Herbert Muller, in his evaluation of the medieval legacy, rises above the more technical aspects of the renaissance problem and presents a perceptive, balanced, gracefully expressed interpretation of the intellectual and cultural achievements of the High Middle Ages (c. 1050–1300). His analysis covers not only the epoch of the "Twelfth-Century Renaissance" but also the generations immediately following, when the dynamic cultural elements forged by the twelfth century were fused into a mature synthesis. Writing from the viewpoint of a modern liberal skeptic, Professor Muller explores both the glories and the limitations of high medieval civilization.

Offhand, even the enduring achievements of medieval men are melancholy reminders of their lost cause. Their cathedrals give Europe its most hallowed charm and dignity but are ghostly in their silence, forlorn in their isolation from the civic life that once swirled through and about them. (A medieval ghost might be more horrified by the tourists strolling their aisles with guidebooks than he was by the lovers who made them a trysting-ground, or the students who played dice on their altars.) Their great universities—one of the most original of their unconscious creations—remain centers of learning, but of a heretical, worldly kind of learning; their "cleric" has dwindled into clerk. Their aristocratic ideals of romantic love have become the stock in trade

SOURCE. Herbert J. Muller, *The Uses of the Past*, New York: Oxford University Press, 1952, pp. 249–255. Copyright 1952 by Oxford University Press. Reprinted by permission of the author and the publisher.

of a vast, vulgar industry, cheap entertainment for the masses they disdained. Offhand, their descendants have made a mockery of all their grandiose aspirations. We might only hope that they sleep well after the fitful fever of their lives; for they grew more despairing as their age waned, and they would hardly be proud of the civilization they sired.

Yet we may be proud of them. We owe our being to their restless striving, their eagerness to experiment and adventure—in particular to the ardor for learning, beauty, and fullness of life that made the twelfth century a profounder, more wonderful renaissance than the official Renaissance. Because we have gone on to build a vastly different world we may forget our kinship, and because we are now prone to their despair we may be seduced by the fond legends of their humble piety; but we owe them something better than sentimental fondness. In a time of confused aims, and much mean endeavor, we may profit by recalling the reality of their idealism, the power of their belief in things unseen. We may escape the easy cynicism that denies such realities, and thereby strengthens the power of unprincipled business and political leaders.

For all its corruptions, Christianity in the Middle Ages was never a mere opium for the masses. It was a truly spiritual force, among the most powerful that have made history. It was the mainspring of the great revival that enabled the barbarians of the West to surge ahead of proud Byzantium. The Gothic cathedrals alone testify to a religious exaltation that has never been surpassed, even in the intensely religious East. Secular life was also enveloped in this exaltation, always colored by it, at times fired by it. The very corruptions intensified the spirituality, for they stirred constant indignation, reawakened conscience, and led men back to purer versions of the Christian ideal. And perhaps the purest was actually realized by St. Francis and his band of brothers, at the turn of the thirteenth century. A century later St. Francis might have been burned at the stake as a heretic, because of his sublime disregard of dogma; but at this moment, which may be considered the apex of the Middle Ages or of Christianity itself, medieval man was able to find the perfect expression for his simple absoluteness, and in the midst of corruption to realize his impossible idealism. The message of St. Francis was pure love and joy—a continuous, radiant spiritual gladness born of a real love for all earthly creatures and things, and an utter indifference to all earthly cares and pains. He forgave God and man for everything, except only the pride of the schoolmen.

St. Francis is not the complete Christian, since he cared nothing for reason, knowledge, and the whole classical heritage. At the same time, he knew nothing of Gregory the Great's terrible fears of the world, the flesh, and the Devil.[1] He could achieve his kind of perfection because by this time medieval men had sufficiently mastered their heritage to take liberties with it. While they retained Gregory's legacy—even elaborating upon it with Germanic and Celtic superstitions, introducing new hordes of gnomes, goblins, witches, and werewolves to a demon-infested world— they also made it over in their own image. To the cult of the Devil they added the complementary cult of the Virgin. To Roman order they brought Germanic ardor and lust for life. They reclaimed patristic Christianity emotionally and imaginatively, through grand symbolism, making poetry of its dogma, realizing in their cathedrals the community of God and man that they so painfully sought to demonstrate in their theology. Their art is the token of their supreme achievement, which was to humanize Christianity. In various ways they approached a religious ideal that could satisfy the whole man, making him at home in both the natural and the social world, fulfilling his needs for truth, beauty, and goodness. If this Christian humanism cannot be called the essence of the medieval spirit, which was always prey to a gross worldliness and a neurasthenic other-worldliness, it was at least a real element of this spirit. For us, I think, it is the most valuable element of the medieval legacy.

An obvious example is the ideal of universality. Although it was a narrower ideal than that of the Roman Stoics, embracing only the true believers, it was less provincial than the patriotic ideal that superseded it. Medieval men tended to regard themselves first of all as Christians; they had their share of local pride and jealousy but relatively little of the violent national prejudice that now splits the West. They were at least free from racial prejudice, persecuting men for their beliefs rather than the color

[1] Pope Gregory I (590–604) cautioned against the dangers of Classical (pagan) learning.

of their skin. The deplorable intolerance they bequeathed was less irrational than modern forms.

No less pertinent is medieval economic theory. As Christians, they naturally considered business a subordinate means to the serious business of the good life, and naturally sought to bring it under the rule of Christian morality. St. Thomas Aquinas, among others, worked out their cardinal principle of the "just price": instead of charging whatever the market will bear, and thereby taking advantage of the needs of fellow-Christians, producers and merchants should charge just enough to cover the costs of their labor. (As R. H. Tawney points out, "the last of the Schoolmen was Karl Marx," for they provided the basis of his labor theory of value.) Later thinkers made the just price more elastic, recognizing the complex variables that affect value, but they still agreed that prices could never be left to the discretion of the seller, since this would simply encourage extortion. They also agreed that speculation, or buying and selling for gain, was an unpardonable sin. They even continued to condemn interest on loans: to extract a guaranteed pound of flesh, without labor of one's own, was contrary to nature, Aristotle, and God. In all this the schoolmen were hopelessly impractical, and seem more so because their theory was so contrary to medieval practice, especially the practice of the papacy. They were naïve enough to believe that business morality might be secured by the mere formulation of sound moral principles. But they were never so naïve as to believe that morality would be promoted, and the good society achieved, by glorifying the profit motive. "If it is proper to insist on the prevalence of avarice and greed in high places," Tawney concludes, "it is not less important to observe that men called these vices by their right names, and had not learned to persuade themselves that greed was enterprise and avarice economy."[2]

Political theory was less humane. While it proclaimed the high

[2] Some respectable types in modern America may find themselves in the lowest circles of Dante's hell. He regarded sins of fraud as worse than sins of violence because they were deliberate and cold-blooded, sins against the mind and soul of man; so he reserved his more horrible punishments for flatterers, seducers, fortune-tellers, hypocrites, evil counselors, et cetera. This company—somewhere below the murderers—would now be swelled by advertisers and publicity men. (Muller's footnote.)

duties of rulers, it provided little freedom for the ruled and little protection against misrule; and St. Thomas himself justified the institution of serfdom on economic grounds. Nevertheless, medieval culture contained the seeds of democracy. They flowered briefly in the Italian city-states, fertilizing the soil of the Renaissance; they produced such enduring growths as the common law and parliamentary institutions of England. The Church, moreover, offered a high career that was open to the lowliest men—at least half of the medieval popes were humbly born. And both clerics and nobles kept pronouncing a stereotyped principle of equality: a highly theoretical equality which they made no effort to realize in social life, and which amounted to little more than the melancholy sentiment that all men are equal before death, but which some common men took seriously. Medieval peasants began to claim rights that the peasants of Byzantium hardly conceived. "At the beginning we were all created equal," proclaimed John Ball;[3] "it is the tyranny of perverse men which has caused slavery to arise, in spite of God's law." Ball was properly hanged, drawn, and quartered, but the authorities could not kill his dream of "equal liberty, equal greatness, equal power."

Even the celebrated religious achievements of the Middle Ages have a humanistic significance that conventional piety has obscured. Art was a far more vital force than it is today because it was not fine art. Gothic art was essentially a folk creation, springing from the common people, expressing a common aspiration and joy in creation; it was not monopolized by an elite. (Hence it seemed "barbarous" to a later age, which set up aristocratic canons of taste and moved art from the workshop to the salon, studio, lecture hall, and finally the museum.) From the outset it broke away from the rigid formalism of Byzantine sacred art, and its progress was toward freedom, exuberance, and naturalism. Sculpture gradually overcame the orthodox suspicion of the evil body; painting took to a realistic treatment of religious subjects. The work of Giotto, the first great painter, expressed a frank pleasure in the flesh and the natural world, and amounted to an open repudiation of asceticism and spiritual abstraction. The more exuberant humanism of the Renaissance was a continuation of the medieval trend, not a sudden rebellion.

3 In the later fourteenth century.

Similarly with medieval theology. While its immediate aim was to establish orthodoxy, and its most apparent accomplishment was the official theology of the Roman Catholic Church, its inspiration was a faith in human reason, and its most significant accomplishment was its contribution to the whole adventure of thought. In spite of themselves, the schoolmen established the value of doubt and even of heresy.

One reason why the Dark Ages[4] were dark was that there was no thought worthy of the name of heresy. With the first glimmerings of light men began to question Gregory the Great's legacy of blind faith. As early as the tenth century Berengar rebelled against authority in the name of reason. (Disunity, one might say, was the first sign of the famed medieval unity.) Then St. Anselm proclaimed his motto, "I believe in order to understand," and made a new effort to understand, producing his noted ontological argument for the existence of God. Peter Abelard was much bolder, maintaining that one can believe only what he understands, and that it is ridiculous to preach to others what one does not understand. With Abelard the renaissance of the twelfth century came into full swing. He discovered that the Church Fathers were not infallible guides, listing in his *Sic et Non*[5] some hundred and fifty propositions on which they flatly contradicted one another. He was nevertheless confident that the true faith was perfectly reasonable, and therefore believed in the positive value of doubt; he thought that even heretics should be reasoned with instead of tortured. Above all, he had a passion for knowledge, insisting that all knowledge was good. He accordingly fell a victim to the pious obscurantism of St. Bernard, the still more impassioned champion of orthodoxy. As a saintly skeptic, Bernard was less horrified by Abelard's specific heresies than by his general assumption that sacred truths should not be accepted unless they are comprehensible; and he got Abelard officially condemned and disgraced. Yet the future belonged to his victim.

Students had flocked to Paris from all over Europe to listen to Abelard. He had much to do with the rise of the University of Paris, which became the great center of theology. Before long

[4] Muller is referring here to the period from about 500 to 1000.
[5] *Yes and No.*

the spiritual progeny of Abelard were poring over Aristotle, who
had been discovered through the translations of heathen Arabs
and Jews. Inflamed by his passion for knowledge, they persisted
in studying Aristotle even though ecclesiastical authorities had
properly condemned his philosophy as heretical. The triumph
of Abelard was sealed when Thomas Aquinas came to the University of Paris. St. Thomas carried to a magnificent conclusion
his effort to substitute rational principles for mere appeal to historic authority. Although he acknowledged that certain revealed
truths, such as the existence of angels, could not have been discovered by reason, he never wavered in his insistence upon making God as rational as he himself was.

St. Thomas began the hard way, with the dangerous admission
that the truth of Christianity or even the existence of God cannot
be taken for granted—it seemed self-evident only because of custom. He supplemented the Platonic intuition inherited by Christian theology with the empirical principle of Aristotle. "The
origin of our knowledge is in sense," he stated, "even of those
things that are above sense." He therefore opposed the teaching
of St. Augustine that knowledge of the natural world is unimportant, or that Scripture tells us all we need to know about it.
"The truth of our faith," he declared, "becomes a matter of
ridicule among the infidels if any Catholic, not gifted with the
necessary scientific learning, presents as a dogma what scientific
scrutiny shows to be false." False ideas about God's handiwork
would naturally lead to false conclusions about God himself.
Believing that Aristotle's philosophy contained the essential truth
about the natural world, St. Thomas made his bold effort to
reconcile it with Christianity. He capped his work by an extra-
ordinarily patient, thorough application of the method of Abelard.
In his *Summa Theologiae,* designed for "beginners," he stated
honestly some ten thousand "Objections" to Christian doctrine,
and as honestly tried to meet them.

For his own age, in short, Thomas Aquinas was a modernist,
or even a radical. Shortly after his death the archbishops of Paris
and Canterbury formally condemned his heretical "materialism";
and it took his Dominican order fifty years of politics to get
him canonized. It is this radical spirit that gives enduring significance to his system. The system was indeed a marvelous syn-

thesis of "science and sanctity," wrought with remarkable zest, patience, and acumen, unsurpassed in the history of thought for its combination of imaginative breadth, intellectual rigor, and loving care in detail; but its equilibrium was even more delicate and precarious than that of the Gothic cathedrals. Later schoolmen pointed out basic inconsistencies, and with the rise of science the whole foundation of the elaborate structure was undermined. Today the philosophy of Aquinas is a kind of historical curiosity for most of those outside the Catholic Church and the University of Chicago; and most ordinary Catholics, if they tried to read him, would likely find much of his thought unintelligible or irrelevant. Yet there is nothing curious or irrelevant about his essential faith—his grand conviction that the true faith could and should embrace all knowledge, all truth from all sources.

Hence the real curiosity—the tragic irony—is that the revolutionary philosophy of St. Thomas Aquinas has become the very symbol and stronghold of conservatism. When the pioneers of science, still informed by a pious spirit, made revolutionary discoveries about God's handiwork, one might have expected the Church of Aquinas to welcome this natural knowledge, or at least to avoid the ridicule of infidels by revising dogmas that "scientific scrutiny shows to be false." Instead, it chose to stand on the dogmas. Though it lost the historic battle that ensued, it continued to betray the spirit of Aquinas by stubbornly resisting the new knowledge. And even more demoralizing than the endless conflict was the deepening confusion. Philosophy, science, and religion, which Aquinas had united, now broke apart and went their separate ways, to produce the hodgepodge of thought and feeling that constitutes the state of mind of most literate Christians today. All in all, the boldness and the integrity of St. Thomas Aquinas provide a melancholy perspective on contemporary Christianity. The orthodox flatly reject the "higher criticism," refusing to permit any rational criticism of the Canon that is the basis of their faith. The liberals suffer from the lack of any consistent philosophy, smuggling in traditional beliefs they wish to preserve by talking of symbolism, but evading the intellectual import duties on their symbols. The modern clergyman, lamented the Reverend Kirsopp Lake, is apt to have "a lower standard of intellectual honesty than would be tolerated in any other profession."

PART TWO

What Happened in the Twelfth Century?

ECONOMIC CHANGE

1 FROM   *Marc Bloch*
                   Feudal Society

Thus far the discussion of the "Twelfth-Century Renaissance" has centered on cultural history. But many historians would point to the economic developments underlying periods of cultural change. The distinguished Renaissance historian Wallace K. Ferguson, for example, has stressed that the most typical culture of the Italian Renaissance was that of cities and urban peoples. "From this point of view," he states, "the Renaissance began when the new urban and secular elements in European culture began to weigh down the balance against the feudal and ecclesiastical elements which had dominated the civilization of the Middle Ages."

Yet the period of the "Twelfth-Century Renaissance" was itself an era of rapid urban and commercial expansion. And some of the most characteristic products of the age—universities, cathedrals, radical piety, Franciscanism, to name but a few—were essentially urban phenomena. The great French medievalist Marc Bloch describes here the immense economic, demographic and territorial growth of high medieval Europe and comments perceptively on its social consequences.

We shall endeavour, in another work, to describe the intensive movement of repopulation which, from approximately 1050 to

SOURCE. Marc Bloch, *Feudal Society*, L. A. Manyon, tr., London. Routledge and Kegan Paul, 1961, pp. 69-71. Copyright 1961 by Routledge and Kegan Paul. Reprinted by permission of Routledge and Kegan Paul, Ltd., and The University of Chicago Press.

1250, transformed the face of Europe: on the confines of the Western world, the colonization of the Iberian plateaux and of the great plain beyond the Elbe; in the heart of the old territories, the incessant gnawing of the plough at forest and wasteland; in the glades opened amidst the trees or the brushwood, completely new villages clutching at the virgin soil; elsewhere, round sites inhabited for centuries, the extension of the agricultural lands through the exertions of the assarters. It will be advisable then to distinguish between the stages of the process and to describe the regional variations. For the moment, we are concerned only with the phenomenon itself and its principal effects.

The most immediately apparent of these was undoubtedly the closer association of the human groups. Between the different settlements, except in some particularly neglected regions, the vast empty spaces thenceforth disappeared. Such distances as still separated the settlements became, in any case, easier to traverse. For powers now arose or were consolidated—their rise being favoured by current demographic trends—whose enlarged horizons brought them new responsibilities. Such were the urban middle classes, which owed everything to trade. Such also were the kings and princes; they too were interested in the prosperity of commerce because they derived large sums of money from it in the form of duties and tolls; moreover they were aware— much more so than in the past—of the vital importance to them of the free transmission of orders and the free movement of armies. The activity of the Capetians towards that decisive turning-point marked by the reign of Louis VI,[1] their aggressions, their domanial policy, their part in the organization of the movement of repopulation, were in large measure the reflection of considerations of this kind—the need to retain control of communications between the two capitals, Paris and Orleans, and beyond the Loire or the Seine to maintain contact with Berry or with the valleys of the Oise and the Aisne. It would seem that while the security of the roads had increased, there was no very notable improvement in their condition; but at least the provision of bridges had been carried much farther. In the course of the twelfth century, how many were thrown over all the rivers of Europe! Finally, a fortunate advance in harnessing methods had the effect, about the same time, of increasing very sub-

[1] A.D. 1108–1137.

stantially the efficiency of horse-transport.

The links with neighbouring civilizations underwent a similar transformation. Ships in ever greater numbers ploughed the Tyrrhenian Sea, and its ports, from the rock of Amalfi to Catalonia, rose to the rank of great commercial centres; the sphere of Venetian trade continually expanded; the heavy wagons of the merchant caravans now followed the route of the Danubian plains. These advances were important enough. But relations with the East had not only become easier and more intimate. The most important fact is that they had changed their character. Formerly almost exclusively an importer, the West had become a great supplier of manufactured goods. The merchandise which it thus shipped in quantity to the Byzantine world, to the Latin or Islamic Levant and even—though in smaller amounts—to the Maghreb, belonged to very diverse categories. One commodity, however, easily dominated all the rest. In the expansion of the European economy in the Middle Ages, cloth played the same vital rôle as did metal and cotton goods in that of nineteenth-century England. If in Flanders, in Picardy, at Bourges, in Languedoc, in Lombardy, and yet other places—for the cloth centres were to be found almost everywhere—the noise of the looms and the throbbing of the fullers' mills resounded, it was at least as much for the sake of foreign markets as for local requirements. And undoubtedly this revolution, which saw our Western countries embarking on the economic conquest of the world by way of the East, is to be explained by a multiplicity of causes and by looking—as far as possible—towards the East as well as towards the West. It is none the less true that it could not have occurred without the demographic changes mentioned above. If the population had not been more numerous than before and the cultivated area more extensive; if the fields—their quality improved by augmented manpower and in particular by more intensive ploughing—had not become capable of yielding bigger and more frequent harvests, how could so many weavers, dyers or cloth-shearers have been brought together in the towns and provided with a livelihood?

The North was conquered, like the East. From the end of the eleventh century Flemish cloth was sold at Novgorod. Little by little, the route of the Russian plains became hazardous and was finally closed. Thenceforward Scandinavia and the Baltic countries turned towards the West. The process of change which was thus set in motion was completed when, in the course of the twelfth century, German merchants took over the Baltic. From that time onwards the ports of the Low Countries, especially Bruges, became the centres where northern products were exchanged not only for those of the West itself but also for merchandise from the East. Strong international links united the two frontiers of feudal Europe by way of Germany and especially through the fairs of Champagne.

Such a well-balanced external trade could not fail to bring a flow of coin and precious metals into Europe and so add substantially to its monetary resources. This relative easing of the currency situation was reinforced—and its effects multiplied—by the accelerated rhythm of circulation. For in the very heart of the West the progress of repopulation, the greater ease of communications, the cessation of the invasions which had spread such an atmosphere of confusion and panic over the Western world, and still other causes which it would take too long to examine here, had led to a revival of commerce.

Let us avoid exaggeration, however. The picture would have to be carefully shaded—by regions and by classes. To live on their own resources remained for long centuries the ideal—though one that was rarely attained—of many peasants and most villages. Moreover, the profound transformations of the economy took place only very gradually. It is significant that of the two essential developments in the sphere of currency, one, the minting of larger pieces of silver much heavier than the *denarius*, appeared only at the beginning of the thirteenth century (and even at that date in Italy alone) and the other, the resumption of the minting of gold coins of an indigenous type, was delayed till the second half of the same century. In many respects, what the second feudal age[2] witnessed was less the disappearance of earlier conditions than their modification. This observation applies to the part played by distance as well as to commerce. But the fact that the kings, the great nobles, and the manorial lords should have been able to begin once more to amass substantial wealth, that wage-earning, sometimes under legal forms clumsily adapted from ancient practices, should have increasingly supplanted other

---

[2] Bloch distinguishes between two "feudal ages," the second of which corresponds roughly to the era of Haskins' Twelfth-Century Renaissance.

methods of remunerating services—these signs of an economy in process of revival affected in their turn, from the twelfth century onwards, the whole fabric of human relations.

Furthermore, the evolution of the economy involved a genuine revision of social values. There had always been artisans and merchants; individuals belonging to the latter class had even been able, here and there, to play an important rôle, though collectively neither group counted for much. But from the end of the eleventh century the artisan class and the merchant class, having become much more numerous and much more indispensable to the life of the community, made themselves felt more and more vigorously in the urban setting. This applies especially to the merchant class, for the medieval economy, after the great revival of these decisive years, was always dominated, not by the producer, but by the trader. It was not for the latter class that the legal machinery of the previous age—founded on an economic system in which they occupied only an inferior place—had been set up. But now their practical needs and their mental attitude were bound to imbue it with a new spirit. Born in the midst of a very loosely-knit society, in which commerce was insignificant and money a rarity, European feudalism underwent a fundamental change as soon as the meshes of the human network had been drawn closer together and the circulation of goods and coin intensified.

2   *Bryce Lyon*
Medieval Real-Estate Developments and Freedom

Professor Bryce Lyon of Brown University, a specialist on northern European institutions in the later Middle Ages, discusses here the connection between medieval land clearance and peasant emancipation.

SOURCE. Bryce Lyon, "Medieval Real-Estate Developments and Freedom," in *American Historical Review*, Vol. LXIII, 1957, pp. 50–59. Copyright 1968 by Bryce Lyon. Reprinted by permission of the author.

For western Europe . . . it may be said that numerous historians have emphasized the interdependence of the medieval economic revival, the sharp rise in the demographic curve, and the extensive land reclamation of the eleventh and twelfth centuries; that some historians have shown the connection between these real estate projects and the economic and legal freedom won by the peasant colonist; and that a few historians have gone on to suggest that the new lands of freedom forced change upon the old seignorial land causing lords to commute labor services in order to hold their tenants. But beyond this point historians have seldom ventured; no one has studied in detail the development of social, economic, legal, and political liberty in areas of land reclamation and its effect upon the common man. Admittedly French historians such as Achille Luchaire, Charles Petit-Dutaillis, and Marc Bloch, have attempted to describe how some of these privileged agrarian communities became rural communes with political rights comparable to the urban commune; how with a unity and a certain amount of administrative *savor faire* born out of economic necessity, they first ordered their economic, social, and legal life, then their parish affairs, and finally bargained or fought their way to the status of commune, in some cases juridically recognized by charter. The evidence is so scant, however, that seldom is the description of this evolution satisfactory. Even for northeastern and southern France, where the evidence is most abundant, the lacunae along the way make it extremely difficult to provide a step-by-step account of the evolution from wilderness to commune. In fact, an examination of the pertinent evidence for western Europe suggests that the fullest documentation for such study comes from medieval Flanders. With his magical sense for asking the right questions and surmizing the correct answers, Pirenne sketched the lines of such an evolution in his *Histoire de Belgique*, but he was never to complete the picture. What follows is primarily an attempt to apply this Pirenne idea to the pertinent early texts found in the Flemish cartularies and registers.

By the early eleventh century a fortuitous coincidence of physical and economic developments combined to make Maritime Flanders, then only a belt of windblown sand and aqueous waste extending from Bourbourg to Antwerp, the center of feverish activity by counts and ecclesiastical establishments to reclaim

land from moor, marsh, dune, and sea. In the ninth century the
North Sea, so geologists and geographers tell us, entered upon
one of its phases of receding water level, ending four centuries
of high water, which in the fifth century had forced the evacua-
tion of Frisians and Saxons. It continued to retreat until the fourteenth century, leaving in its wake sand banks, dunes, marshes,
and small streams. Thus smiled upon by Neptune, the Flemish
were able to complete what nature had begun. Through extensive diking and draining, they opened up new land to receive a
growing population and to supply food for the towns sprouting
up in this sensitive economic region. The counts, who possessed
this waste area by virtue of regalian rights usurped from the
Carolingians, began to exploit it directly or to grant parts of it
to be reclaimed by such abbeys as Saint Pierre of Ghent and
Saint-Bertin of Saint-Omer. As early as the eleventh century,
some time between 1055 and 1067, the archbishop of Rheims
wrote a letter to Count Baldwin V congratulating him on having
transformed unproductive waste into fertile lands. In the twelfth
and thirteenth centuries the fight against the sea continued with
the counts and the Cistercians playing the leading role.

But let us see more concretely how this battle was fought. Ten
kilometers south of Dunkerque is the French town of Bergues,
which in the Middle Ages belonged to the county of Flanders.
A wettish place by any standard, averaging 134 days of rainfall
yearly, it was even soggier in the early Middle Ages. In the fifth
century it was but a speck in the sea connected to the continent
by a ribbon of land. This ribbon had widened by the tenth century, and the elevation of land known as Mont Saint-Winnoc
was surrounded on three sides by marsh. On the seaward side,
however, water continued to lap at the tip of the finger of land
and was still doing so in the year 1107. It was here that some of
the first extensive land reclamation occurred. In 1067 Count
Baldwin V issued a remarkable charter to the Benedictine monastery of Bergues-Saint-Winnoc. Proudly stating in the preamble
that it had been founded by his predecessor Baldwin the Bald
(879 918), he showed his benevolent attitude toward the monastery by bestowing on it a goodly number of revenues, rights,
and land. Saint-Winnoc was to receive reclaimed land just to the
south at Wormhout and, in addition, all the dunes at Synthes and

any land that would accrue there by the shifting of the sea. It was also empowered to exploit any land reclaimed from the sea and marsh. To ensure the labor necessary for such an enterprise, Baldwin provided that all *hospites*[1] who came there were to be free from all seignorial obligations, exempt from *taille*[2] and arbitrary exaction, and free from the *ban*[3] and service owed to count or *châtelain*.[4] Baldwin then defined the nature of the relations between the *hospites* and the abbot. They were to enjoy the same status as the comital *hospites* who were under the jurisdiction of the *prévôt*[5] and *échevins*[6] of the *châtellenie*[7] of Bruges, that is, they were to be subject to officers appointed by the abbot. Though the charter is not too explicit, it would seem that each settler was to pay 6*d*. annually for his land, which could be passed on to heirs. At the end Baldwin swore to protect the men of Saint-Winnoc as he would his own subjects. Here, at one stroke, was created an agrarian *ville neuve*[8] with most of the elementary bourgeois privileges held by the inhabitants of such towns as Ghent, Bruges, and Saint-Omer which, as yet, had not attained communal status. Wasteland continued to be granted to Saint-Winnoc in the twelfth and thirteenth centuries, and the privileged land of freedom around it constantly expanded as plot after plot of land was won from water and converted into pasture and arable land.

At Bourbourg, a few kilometers to the west of Saint-Winnoc, was the Benedictine house of Notre-Dame, a convent for women founded in 1101 by Count Robert II. Immediately upon its founding it received grants and favors from the comital house, and before long Robert bestowed upon it certain donations and privileges. It was to receive some newly won land just to the west at Bonehem and whatever land should be reclaimed from

[1] Peasants holding by customary tenure.
[2] Tallage: a tax.
[3] General summons to arms.
[4] Castellan: the keeper of a castle or lord of a district surrounding a castle.
[5] Provost: a local officer.
[6] The modern "alderman": a local officer.
[7] Castelry: a territory under the jurisdiction of a castellan. See above, note 4.
[8] "New town"; many territorial lords of the period were establishing "new towns" with rights and privileges sufficient to attract new burghers.

the sea by poldering. The settlers were to hold their land heritably and upon inheritance to pay a nominal relief. All were obliged to guard and repair the dikes, but if the sea should inundate the land through no fault of theirs, the convent would pay for reconstructing the dikes. All justice was to reside with the convent. A sheepfold called *terra nova*, not far from Furnes along the Yser River, was given to the convent. In addition, it was to receive any land won from the sea. When reclaimed and measured into plots, the land was to be assessed rents by experienced men of the community. We need not delve into the rest of the charter dealing with the payment of rents and dike obligations to see that the settlers in these two regions were to enjoy the same elementary bourgeois liberties as the *hospites* who extended the comital domains.

Much of our information concerning the comital *hospites* comes from a charter granted by Count Robert II (1093–1111) to his men of Berquin and Steenwerck, two areas lying near the stream of Estaires in the moors to the southeast of Ypres. The men paid a yearly rent of grain for their land and were freed from all seignorial exactions and from military service. They were empowered to elect a magistrate who was to render justice in the presence of the seneschal of the count. If the magistrate was unjust, they could replace him; if the comital *châtelain* or any such officer oppressed them, they could appeal to the count for justice. A charter granted by Thierry of Alsace in 1161, some sixty years later, supplements our knowledge of the privileged status of the comital *hospites*. He granted to settlers for cultivation his *solitudino*, a moor area around the present village of Woesten (wasteland), ten kilometers northwest of Ypres. They were to be entirely free from all seignorial services and exactions and from public services save for the common defense of the land. Thierry promised to build a church for the settlers, guaranteeing that it would be a separate parish. They were to be subject only to the authority and justice of the count and his delegated officer, in this instance the *notarius*[9] of Ypres. No one could be tried other than in the local court presided over by the *notarius*, who was to receive twice yearly at Ypres a rent of money and kind from the settlers for their parcels of land.

[9] Notary.

And so it went with other communities. In 1107 Nieuport began its existence on a piece of land reclaimed from the sea at Sandeshove at the mouth of the Yser; poldering continued and in 1163 Count Thierry founded there a *ville neuve* with the customary elementary bourgeois privileges. To the west and east arose Dunkerque, East Dunkerque, Westende, Middelkerke, Ostende, and Blankenberge. Inland there were Furnes, Dixmude, Ramskapelle, and Westkerke. Along the Zwin River from Bruges to the sea the development was particularly striking. The Zwin, originally a gulf extending up to Bruges, had shrunk to a narrow river in the twelfth century and then silted rapidly as the sea kept withdrawing and poldering along its banks progressed. Damme appeared first, in 1150, located on new land of the count of Flanders. In 1200 we hear of Mude, which by 1226 was a port. Also in 1226 the records first speak of Monnikerede. In the middle of the century Hoeke appeared, and then later Sluis. These foundations soon became prominent ports with elementary bourgeois liberties. Meanwhile, all about the *châtellenie* of Bruges and in the Quatre-Métiers next to the Scheldt reclamation produced scores of small free agrarian communities such as Lisseweghe, Westkapelle, and Watervliet. Those strategically located for trade quickly sloughed off their agrarian character and became urban marts or ports; the others remained agricultural villages, as is the case even today with many such as Lisseweghe and Woesten.

These examples spell out in detail how the counts and ecclesiastical establishments cooperated to convert Maritime Flanders from a desolate waste into a fertile, revenue producing land peopled with free farmers living in an economically, socially, and legally privileged area. They lacked only self-government; but even it was to come soon. The ingredients necessary to secure it—communal unity and cooperation in economic and legal affairs—were present from the outset. To win land from the sea and to hold it, dike associations were organized with officers and regulations. In spite of a lack of evidence in the twelfth century on the organization of such cooperative enterprises, we know that they existed, first as independent local creations and then as associations centrally supervised by comital officers. From the early thirteenth century these associations appear in the texts under the name of *Wateringen* and, as such, they still exist in Maritime Flanders. In the territorial constitution of Flanders the *Water ingen* are analogous to the urban guilds which took the lead in winning self-government for communes such as Saint-Omer and Bruges. Organized as was the guild merchant to meet an economic need, these associations became autonomous corporations and instruments of public power. . . . These, then, were the organizations that came in the late twelfth and thirteenth centuries to bargain with counts for self-government, a goal they, like the famous communes of the early twelfth century, attained by peaceful negotiation with enlightened rulers.

In 1180 Damme attained its *échevinage*[10] and a charter of liberties modeled upon that of Bruges. Around the middle of the thirteenth century Mude, Monikerede, and Hoeke received the liberties of Bruges, as did Sluis in 1290. Turning to the west, we find that Nieuport was self-governing in the early thirteenth century, that Ostende followed suit in 1267. During the thirteenth century all the prominent communities, that is, those that rapidly developed into commercial centers, attained a similar status. But particularly significant is the number of small communities of free, self-reliant farmers that acquired self-government in the thirteenth century—Watervliet, Eecloo, Aardenbourg, and Ysendike. There is some reason to believe that the free farmers of Oudenbourg, a small farming community just west of Bruges, used the disturbances connected with the assassination of Count Charles the Good in 1127 to acquire self-government along with Saint-Omer, Bruges, and the other large towns. Still but a tiny farming village, Oudenbourg exemplifies the small agrarian villages that secured self-government in the twelfth and thirteenth centuries and then remained rural communities or, as they are termed, rural communes down to the end of the *Ancien Régime*.

By 1300 the administrative circumscriptions that composed Maritime Flanders—the Franc de Bruges, the *châtellenies* of Furnes, Bergues, Cassel, Bailleul, Bourbourg, and Bruges—had become territorial communes. The urban communes remained independent from territorial organization and dealt directly with the

---

[10] Status of being a separate self-governing political unit under an *échevin* or alderman. See note 6.

counts or the *baillis*,[11] but the rural communities were lumped together into a territorial arrangement forming a vast commune. A group of *échevins* composed a territorial court and an administrative council; associated with this territorial *échevinage* were the *échevins* of the small rural communities. Each territorial commune enjoyed the same status as the great towns: each possessed its law, its privileges, and its court; each enjoyed a large autonomy and constituted a corporation recognized and guaranteed by public law. . . .

But what relevance do these developments have for the rest of Europe? Maritime Flanders, composed almost entirely of land won from water or waste, never knew seignorialism. Consequently, beginning with the eleventh century, it formed a privileged area that wore down the seignorial system dominant in the interior of Flanders. So relentless was the competition of this free land against the seignorial system that it forced early and rapid commutation of labor services. In 1252 . . . Countess Margaret . . . virtually proclaimed the end of serfdom in the county of Flanders and was only giving legal recognition to an economic situation that had existed in much of Flanders since the early thirteenth century.

The pattern is the same in other comparable areas of *défrichement*[12] and reclamation. None of Maritime Holland had known seignorialism, and in the interior it had never been widespread. The seignorial system had no part in the great expanses brought under cultivation in Germany during the twelfth and thirteenth centuries; this is strikingly evident in northern Germany, particularly in the Ems, Weser, and Elbe region. Delisle and others have proven that Artois, Pontieu, Picardy, and Normandy, where the earliest and most vigorous *défrichement* and reclamation occurred, saw the early disappearance of serfdom and the rise of free agrarian communities, many of them rural communes. The same is true for the *bastide* region.

Though observations for England are hampered by lack of research on the subject, there must be some connection between the large number of free farmers in thirteenth- and fourteenth-century Lincolnshire, Cambridgeshire, Essex, and Kent and the

[11] Bailiff: an important comital or royal official.
[12] Land clearing.

land reclamation found in these counties from an early time. This definitely is the case around the estuary of the Thames; the area surrounding the Wash, especially Holland in Lincolnshire; Romney Marsh; and the fens. It thus seems reasonable to conclude that agrarian freedom began first in these real estate developments and then fermented the commutation of labor services on seignorial land. Furthermore, it is safe to say that the constant pressure of these free areas guaranteed no letup in the commutation nor any retrogression to seignorialism. In the light of what Michael Postan has told us about the chronology of labor services in thirteenth-century England, that commutation dropped to insignificant proportions and that there was a widespread attempt to reintroduce seignorial obligations, this remark may seem curious. But Postan's conclusions are questionable for the areas of reclamation. There, free men increased, and in areas closely adjacent, commutation of services continued. Because of these islands of freedom there could be no retrogression; there could be only progression. It is contended, therefore, that in many parts of Europe the free reclaimed lands exerted a constant and powerful pressure for the emancipation of the common man, and that they achieved this result much earlier than could have been done by the commutation of labor services alone.

3 FROM THE

Charter of the Rural Commune of Lorris

The following excerpts are from a charter of privileges such as Professor Lyon referred to frequently in the previous article. The privileges of the small agrarian district of Lorris (reign of Louis VI, 1108–1137) in the Île de France became a model for numerous subsequent charters.

SOURCE. Frederick A. Ogg, ed., *A Source Book of Mediaeval History*, New York: American Book Company, 1907, pp. 328–330. Reprinted by permission of American Book Company.

1. Every one who has a house in the parish of Lorris shall pay as *cens* sixpence only for his house, and for each acre of land that he possesses in the parish.[1]

2. No inhabitant of the parish of Lorris shall be required to pay a toll or any other tax on his provisions; and let him not be made to pay any measurage fee on the grain which he has raised by his own labor.

3. No burgher shall go on an expedition, on foot or on horseback, from which he cannot return the same day to his home if he desires.[2]

4. No burgher shall pay toll on the road to Étampes, to Orleans, to Milly (which is in the Gâtinais), or to Melun.

5. No one who has property in the parish of Lorris shall forfeit it for any offense whatsoever, unless the offense shall have been committed against us or any of our *hôtes*.[3]

6. No person while on his way to the fairs and markets of Lorris, or returning, shall be arrested or disturbed, unless he shall have committed an offense on the same day.[4]

9. No one, neither we nor any other, shall exact from the burghers of Lorris any tallage, tax, or subsidy.[5]

[1] This trifling payment of sixpence a year was made in recognition of the lordship of the king, the grantor of the charter. Aside from it, the burgher had full rights over his land. (This and the subsequent footnotes to the Charter of Lorris are Professor Ogg's.)

[2] The object of this provision is to restrict the amount of military service due the king. The burghers of small places like Lorris were farmers and traders who made poor soldiers and who were ordinarily exempted from service by their lords. The provision for Lorris practically amounted to an exemption, for such service as was permissible under chapter 3 of the charter was not worth much.

[3] This protects the landed property of the burghers against the crown and crown officials. With two exceptions, fine or imprisonment, not confiscation of land, is to be the penalty for crime. *Hôtes* denotes persons receiving land from the king and under his direct protection.

[4] This provision is intended to attract merchants to Lorris by placing them under the king's protection and assuring them that they would not be molested on account of old offenses.

[5] This chapter safeguards the personal property of the burghers, as chapter 5 safeguards their land. Arbitrary imposts are forbidden and any of the inhabitants who as serfs had been paying arbitrary tallage are relieved of the burden. The nominal *cens* (Chap. 1) was to be the only regular payment due the king.

12. If a man shall have had a quarrel with another, but without breaking into a fortified house, and if the parties shall have reached an agreement without bringing a suit before the provost, no fine shall be due to us or our provost on account of the affair.[6]

15. No inhabitant of Lorris is to render us the obligation of *corvée*,[7] except twice a year, when our wine is to be carried to Orleans, and not elsewhere.

16. No one shall be detained in prison if he can furnish surety that he will present himself for judgment.

17. Any burgher who wishes to sell his property shall have the privilege of doing so; and, having received the price of the sale, he shall have the right to go from the town freely and without molestation, if he so desires, unless he has committed some offense in it.

18. Any one who shall dwell a year and a day in the parish of Lorris, without any claim having pursued him there, and without having refused to lay his case before us or our provost, shall abide there freely and without molestation.

35. We ordain that every time there shall be a change of provosts in the town the new provost shall take an oath faithfully to observe these regulations; and the same thing shall be done by new sergeants every time that they are installed.

4   *Otto of Freising*
 On the Lombard Communes

These excerpts from the important twelfth-century historian Otto of Freising illustrate some of the characteristics of the new towns and townsmen. The urban revolution was particularly intense in Lombardy where the cities entered into a league against their nominal overlord, the Holy Roman Emperor. Otto of Freising, a subject and admirer of Emperor Frederick Barbarossa, discloses a distinct hos-

---

[6] An agreement outside of court was allowable in all cases except when there was a serious breach of the public peace.

[7] Work service to the lord (C. W. H.).

tility toward the independence-minded Lombard townsmen. In gen-
eral, Otto is observing the twelfth-century urban revolution in Lom-
bardy from the viewpoint of the German aristocratic-ecclesiastical
landed élite.

But [the Lombards] having put aside crude, barbarous ferocity, perhaps from the fact that when united in marriage with the natives they begat sons who inherited something of the Roman gentleness and keenness from their mothers' blood, and from the very quality of the country and climate, retain the refinement of the Latin speech and their elegance of manners. In the governing of their cities, also, and in the conduct of public affairs, they still imitate the wisdom of the ancient Romans. Finally, they are so desirous of liberty that, avoiding the insolence of power, they are governed by the will of consuls rather than rulers. There are known to be three orders among them: captains, vavasors, and commoners. And in order to suppress arrogance, the aforesaid consuls are chosen not from one but from each of the classes. And lest they should exceed bounds by lust for power, they are changed almost every year. The consequence is that, as practically that entire land is divided among the cities, each of them requires its bishops to live in the cities, and scarcely any noble or great man can be found in all the surrounding territory who does not acknowledge the authority of his city. And from this power to force all elements together they are wont to call the several lands of each [noble, or magnate] their contado (*comitatus*).[1] Also, that they may not lack the means of subduing their neighbors, they do not disdain to give the girdle of knighthood or the grades of distinction to young men of inferior station and even some workers of the vile mechanical arts, whom other peoples bar like the pest from the more respected and honorable pursuits. From this it has resulted that they far surpass all other states of the world in riches and in power. They are aided in this

[1] Literally "county."

SOURCE. Otto of Freising, *Deeds of Frederick Barbarossa*, C. C. Mierow and Richard Emery, trs., in *Records of Civilization*, No. XLIX, New York; Columbia University Press, 1953, pp. 127–129. Copyright 1953 by Columbia University Press. Reprinted by permission of Columbia University Press.

not only, as has been said, by their characteristic industry, but also by the absence of their princes,[2] who are accustomed to remain on the far side of the Alps. In this, however, forgetful of their ancient nobility, they retain traces of their barbaric imperfection, because while boasting that they live in accordance with law, they are not obedient to the laws. For they scarcely if ever respect the prince to whom they should display the voluntary deference of obedience or willingly perform that which they have sworn by the integrity of their laws, unless they sense his authority in the power of his great army. Therefore it often happens that although a citizen must be humbled by the laws and an adversary subdued by arms in accordance with the laws, yet they very frequently receive in hostile fashion him whom they ought to accept as their own gentle prince, when he demands what is rightfully his own. From this arises a twofold loss to the common weal: the prince is obliged to assemble an army for the subjugation of his people, and the people (not without great loss of their own possessions) are forced to obey their prince. Accordingly, by the same process of reasoning whereby impetuosity accuses the people for this situation, so should necessity excuse the prince in the sight of God and men.

Among all the cities of this people Milan now holds chief place. It is situated between the Po and Pyrenees, and between the Ticino and the Adda, which take their source from the same Pyrenees and drain into the Po, thereby creating a certain very fertile valley, like an island. Located midway, it is rightly called *Mediolanum*, although some think it was named *Mediolanum* by its founders from a certain portentous sow that had bristles on one side and wool on the other. Now this city is considered (as has been said) more famous than others not only because of its size and its abundance of brave men, but also from the fact that it has extended its authority over two neighboring cities situated within the same valley, Como and Lodi. Furthermore—as usually happens in our transitory lot when favoring fortune smiles— Milan, elated by prosperity, became puffed up to such audacious exaltation that not only did it not shrink from molesting its neighbors, but recently even dared incur the anger of the prince, standing in no awe of his majesty.

2 The Holy Roman Emperors.

POLITICAL INSTITUTIONS AND
POLITICAL THEORY

5   *C. H. McIlwain*
          Medieval Institutions in the Modern World

Professor McIlwain, a distinguished authority in the field of medieval political theory, discusses here the relationship between the political institutions of high medieval Europe and those of the modern world.

. . . There is the view that the thirteenth century is, as it has been called, "the greatest of Christian centuries"; and, on the other hand, the notion, widespread a generation ago if not now, that the Renaissance was a "rediscovery of the world and of man." What shall we believe about that? For these two views are irreconcilable. No doubt historians as far removed from our time as we are from the Middle Ages will have somewhat the same conflicting opinions about the first half of the twentieth century. Even today we find some saying that these moving times are a great time to be alive, while others can only look back with longing to an earlier period when rights and honor and oaths were at least respected, even if not always observed.

With such a disparity of opinions about the present, how can

SOURCE. C. H. McIlwain, "Medieval Institutions in the Modern World," in *Speculum*, Vol. XVI, 1941, pp. 276–278 and 280–283. Copyright 1941 by *Speculum*. Reprinted by permission of *Speculum*.

we be surprised to find them in regard to the Middle Ages? Our definitions of the mediaeval, like those of the present, will be affected by our temperament, our traditions, and our peculiar studies. The best definition we can frame will be partial, incomplete, and inadequate; and the sum of all these defects will probably be the result of ignorance of something essential.

Sometimes the present-day exhibitions of this ignorance become almost grotesque. I quote: "Another result of the low level of civilization and culture in the Middle Ages was the total absence of a scientific attitude. People blindly accepted on the authority of others their beliefs and their rules of conduct. . . . They never questioned the accuracy of these interpretations, never tried to think things out for themselves." I regret to say that the quotation I have just given comes from a textbook now or recently used very widely in many schools in the United States. If children continue to be fed on books by writers of such appalling ignorance as this, we may well despair, not only of the past but of the future. The days of any Mediaeval Academy of America will certainly be numbered.

The horrible quotation I have just made is an indication of another characteristic commonly believed to be true of the Middle Ages: it is supposed to be a period of more or less complete stagnation. "Progress" is thought to be solely a modern achievement. But could anyone put Isidore of Seville's *Etymologies* beside the great *Summa* of St. Thomas Aquinas and say there was no intellectual progress between the seventh century and the thirteenth?

The discriminating historian will not fall in with these extremes, certainly not with those of the sentimentalists who see in the Middle Ages no less than a Golden Age, and in modern times nothing good that is not mediaeval. For such a view the disclosure of the seamy side of mediaeval life in the authentic contemporary records of the courts of law is a valuable antidote, or some of the chronicles of the time, or the realism of a Luchaire or a Coulton.[1] But the crass ignorance of the opposite view is infinitely worse, the view that the Middle Age is an epoch of

[1] A selection from G. G. Coulton is included later in this book (Part Two, Reading 28).

unmitigated barbarism. It would certainly be unfair to base an estimate of our present-day civilization solely on a study of the records of the police courts, and for the Middle Ages this kind of document has survived in greater quantity than most others. But most people never get into a police court today, and most people did not in the Middle Ages. The mass of surviving judicial records, in some places so extensive when compared with other kinds of records, should not give us a distorted notion of the prevalence of violence or litigiousness at the time. Such records have survived in some places almost by the ton. We are likely to forget that the quiet lives of the bulk of the people, then as now, would leave no trace in the records of any court, either criminal or civil. But on the other side of the scale, it is just as necessary to bear in mind that the grandeur of the cathedrals which put us in awe today is not a proof of the universality of mediaeval piety.

The period that we dub mediaeval is a long one, and on that side of it in which my own studies have lain I think we find, within the period itself, changes as profound, if not even more profound, than those which mark off our modern institutions from the ones we call mediaeval. In the field of political institutions and ideas I venture to think that what Professor Haskins has termed "the Renaissance of the twelfth century" marks a more fundamental change than the later developments to which we usually attach the word "Renaissance"; that the constitutionalism of the modern world owes as much, if not even more, to the twelfth and the thirteenth centuries than to any later period of comparable length before the seventeenth.

All this is to do little more than say that the term "Middle Ages" in its widest extent is a term which includes institutions and ideas as widely different from each other as the so-called mediaeval is from the modern. If so, which of them shall we term "mediaeval" *par excellence?* Or shall we give it all up, and say that all we dare do is to term "mediaeval" anything and everything we find in the whole millennium generally included under the phrase "Middle Ages"? Pitfalls certainly do lie in the path of anyone who is looking for the peculiar flavor of the Middle Ages, and many there are who have fallen in. In my own field

I am thinking particularly of historians such as Freeman,[2] who became so obsessed by the notion of constitutional liberty as the dominant note of mediaeval political life that he could never see the feudalism that everywhere stared him in the face, or, if he saw it, could only damn it as an abuse. He had a pattern ready-made to which the institutions of the time must conform.

There have been many like patterns. Another such is the notion that a more or less complete decentralization of government is a characteristic necessarily inherent in the Middle Ages; and therefore, if we find a strong monarchy somewhere in the midst of the mediaeval period, that we must not call it mediaeval; it must be an aberration. But because we find that so many of these patterns do not truly fit the existing facts, must we conclude that after all there is nothing whatever whose character warrants us in attaching to it the adjective "mediaeval"? Is there no distinctive mediaeval pattern at all? Or further, is there nothing in our modern culture that we may safely trace back in unbroken continuity into the mediaeval period and term a mediaeval heritage?

In the attempt to list a few things that seem at the same time mediaeval and modern, I shall not venture to touch anything but the field of political institutions and ideas, beyond which my knowledge is mainly but second-hand. And in making even such a tentative list I think we must always bear in mind the vast difference between the earlier and the later part of the long period to which we apply the word "mediaeval." As a whole, I suppose we might roughly describe the epoch generally as one in which rather primitive men gradually and progressively assimilated the more advanced institutions and ideas that antiquity had bequeathed them. It is amazing how long a period of contact it required for men at such a primitive state of culture to make their own the remains of a civilization so much higher than theirs. In western Europe one can hardly make this period of progressive assimilation shorter than seven or eight centuries. It was a long, gradual, progressive development, a slow evolution; and the term "mediaeval" is probably most fittingly applied to the culmination in its later centuries, on Aristotle's general teleological principle

---

[2] E. A. Freeman, an English medievalist of the nineteenth century, whose best known work is the multivolumed *History of the Norman Conquest.*

that the nature of any developing thing is only fully knowable in the final outcome of that development.

One of the things, probably the most important of all the things in my own particular field, that we seem to owe in largest part to these developments of the Middle Ages, is the institution of limited government, which I take to be the synonym for constitutionalism.

This constitutionalism was, of course, no new thing when the mediaeval records of it first appear. It had been a characteristic of republican Rome, had never been wholly obliterated by the growing absolutism of the Empire, and it was enshrined in the Roman legal sources which the ruder successors of the Romans inherited and gradually came in course of time to assimilate, understand, and apply to their own lives. More and more I have become impressed lately with the relative importance of this Roman influence upon the mediaeval growth of our own principles of political liberty; an importance that political developments since the Middle Ages have tended to obscure, and one that it has been the usual fashion of the historians of our laws and constitutions to belittle, to ignore, or even to deny. The recent repudiation of Roman law by the Nazis in Germany because it is inconsistent with their totalitarianism makes one wonder if we have not, for a long time, been greatly over-emphasizing the despotic influence of that law in our history, and as seriously under-rating the importance of Roman constitutionalism in the early development of our own. . . .

In coming, then, at this long last, to the subject I am supposed to talk about, the mediaeval in the present, this subject of Roman law furnishes one good example. In England and America at least, we have on the whole been prone to accept without enough examination the thesis that on its political side Roman law in the Middle Ages was but a prop to absolutism. We have usually taken at its face value the assertion of Sir John Fortescue, near the end of the fifteenth century, that the absolutist doctrines contained in such maxims as *"quod principi placuit legis vigorem habet,"*[3] or Ulpian's statement *"princeps legibus solutus est"*[4] ex-

---

3 "Whatever pleases the prince has the force of law."
4 "The prince is free of the laws."

press "the chief principles among the civil laws" . . . as he called
them. To one who has accepted this tradition without much question it is something of a shock to look back to the thirteenth century and learn that Bracton[5] sees nothing whatsoever of this kind
in Roman law.

Once started on such an investigation, the student soon finds
that thirteenth-century men generally, unlike those of the fifteenth or the sixteenth, found no absolutism in the law of Rome,
but rather constitutionalism. Such absolutist statements as the ones
above do not for Bracton express the true central principle either
of Roman or of English politics. That central principle is rather
to be found in Papinian's dictum "Lex est communis sponsio rei
publicae,"[6] "the common engagement of the republic," not "the
pleasure of the prince." And in this, the mediaeval conception
of the political side of Roman law is typical of mediaeval political
ideas generally. To men of the thirteenth century Roman political principles and their own seemed essentially alike, not unlike;
and neither the Roman nor their own were despotic. In proof of
this, other passages of Roman law might easily be cited in addition
to the ones we have already noted.

In our own earlier history there is, for example, the famous
extract in Edward I's writ of summons to the Parliament of 1295,
in which the Archbishop of Canterbury is enjoined, before appearing himself, to secure the presence in person or by deputy
of the lower clergy of his province: . . . "As a most just law,
established by the far-sighted wisdom of sacred princes urges and
has ordained that what touches all should be approved by all;
equally and most clearly [it implies] that common dangers should
be met by remedies provided in common." In its original use, as
repeated in Justinian's Code, this provision has to do only with
the private law, but it is here used as a maxim of state in a matter
of the highest political importance. It is true that some have
regarded Edward I's quotation of it as of very little significance,
and Professor G. B. Adams even cites its frequent use in earlier
ecclesiastical documents as proof of this; but to me this repeated

---

[5] A great thirteenth-century English jurist and author of the treatise, Of
the Laws and Customs of England.
[6] "Law is the common engagement of the republic."

quotation is an indication not of its unimportance, but rather of the wide prevalence in mediaeval politics of the idea it expresses.

Modern interpretations of this famous writ have usually failed to notice its emphasis on the inference to be drawn from Justinian's words, as expressed in the added clause "that common dangers should be met by remedies provided in common." This added clause contains the kernel of the writ, and indicates the royal purpose in calling up the extraordinary number of the lower clergy. . . . It was very natural and very effective, in a writ summoning the clergy to an assembly in which a large grant was to be asked for, thus to cite in justification a maxim which the clergy themselves had used so long and so often in their own provincial assemblies. The political idea underlying this maxim finds constant expression, not only in the words of the thirteenth century, in England, in France, and in many other parts of western Europe; but in the institutions as well.

It is to such institutions that I should like in the next place to turn as a further example of the mediaeval in its influence upon the modern. It is a commonplace of modern constitutional history that the power of the purse has been the principal means of securing and maintaining the liberties of the subject against the encroachments of the prince. Probably in no part of our constitutional history is the influence of the Middle Ages upon the modern world more obvious than here. For the constitutional principle just mentioned can be shown to be the outgrowth, the gradual and at times almost unperceived outgrowth, of the mediaeval principle that a feudal lord in most cases can exact no aid from his vassal save with the consent of all like vassals of the same fief. The whole principle contained in our maxim, "no taxation without representation," has this feudal practice as its origin.

This is probably so obvious and so generally admitted that it needs little proof or illustration. But one aspect of it we are likely to overlook. These rights of the vassal are proprietary rights, and we are likely to give them a definition as narrow as our own modern definition of proprietary rights. This, however, is to misinterpret the nature of these limitations and vastly to lessen the importance of the principle of consent in the Middle Ages. For these rights of vassals, though protected by what we should call

the land-law, included almost all of those rights which today we
term "personal," such as the right to office, the right to immuni-
ties, or, as they were usually called then, to "liberties" or fran-
chises, and even to the right to one's security in his social and
personal status. A serf, for example, was protected against the
abuse by his lord of rights which we call "personal" by remedies
which it is difficult to distinguish from those used for the protection of the seisin of land. One might be truly said to have been
"seized" of the rights securing his person as much as of those
protecting his fief. It may be said of the Middle Ages generally
then, that private rights were immune from governmental en-
croachment under the political principles of the time. In this the
Middle Ages shared the principles of Roman Law, and no doubt
it was this common feature of both systems that enabled Glanvil
and Bracton and all the jurists in the period between to liken the
English Law in so many respects to the Roman.

If we are estimating the importance of the mediaeval in the
modern in this field from which I have chosen to illustrate it,
this constitutionalism, this limitation of governmental authority
by private right, is the main tradition handed down by the Middle Ages to the modern world. It is the chief element in the
political part of our mediaeval heritage. With the decay of feudal
institutions, however, the sanctions by which these principles
were maintained in practice tended to be greatly weakened, and
no doubt it is the lawlessness of this later period of weakness following the decay of the feudal and preceding the development
of the national sanctions for law, which has led to the popular
impression that the Middle Ages as a whole are nothing more
than one long stretch of uncontrolled violence. No doubt the
violence of this later period may also be considered to be the
chief cause of the increasing power of monarchy and the almost
unlimited theories of obedience which we find among the chief
characteristics of the period of the Renaissance. As was said then,
it is better to submit to one tyrant than to a thousand. And without doubt the weakness of these sanctions of law in the later
Middle Ages is a prime cause of the strength of monarchy in the
period immediately following. In the reaction and revolution
which in time were provoked in the period of the Renaissance

or afterward by the extension and abuse of these powers of government we may find the true causes of the modern sanctions for the subjects' rights. In the early stages at least of this revolution the precedents cited in favor of liberty are largely drawn from the Middle Ages.

The particular side of the Middle Ages with which we have been dealing certainly offers little proof of either of the extreme interpretations that we find in modern times. It was both a lawful and a lawless period. At no time was law more insisted upon, but at times few of these laws were observed. When we consider this period in comparison with periods following, the same discrimination is necessary. The political theory of that time included more limitations upon governmental power than many theories of a much later time. It may indeed be said that political absolutism, at least as a theory of government, is a modern and not a mediaeval notion. In fact, the great champions of liberty against oppression, if their own words are to be trusted, have fought for the maintenance of liberties inherited from the Middle Ages. In our own day such traditional conceptions of liberty appear less seldom perhaps, for many liberals, and certainly most extreme radicals, are now frequently struggling for rights for which the Middle Ages can furnish few precedents. But this should not blind us to the all-important fact that for a long period in this historic struggle; indeed for the whole of the early part of it, it was for their mediaeval inheritance that all opponents of oppression engaged.

The lesson of it all is discrimination. If some modern elements had not been added to our mediaeval inheritance, elements nonexistent before modern times, even that inheritance could scarcely have persisted; and yet the central principle for which free men have always fought, the sanctity of law against oppressive will, is a principle recognized by our medieval ancestors as fully as by ourselves, and more fully, apparently, than by their successors of the sixteenth century. We cannot, therefore, truly entertain notions of the Middle Ages which make it one long, dreary epoch of stagnation, of insecurity, of lawless violence; neither can we truly consider it the Golden Age that some have pictured. What we need above all is discrimination and yet more discrimination.

6   *John of Salisbury*
            On Tyranny and Tyrannicide

*The constitutionalism which Professor McIlwain found implicit
in the medieval institutions of feudalism and limited monarchy is expressed at the theoretical level in, among other things, the distinction
between kingship and tyranny. A king—or prince—was bound to gov-
ern lawfully. A ruler who placed himself above law was no king but
a tyrant, and a tyrant need not be obeyed. This distinction between
king and tyrant recurs in the writings of medieval political theorists.
In this passage the great twelfth-century English humanist John of
Salisbury addresses himself to the difficult problem of how a subject
might resist a tyrant and hesitantly suggests the solution of political
assassination or "tyrannicide." Note that John of Salisbury draws his
arguments from a comprehensive knowledge of Roman and Biblical
literature.*

Wherein the prince differs from the tyrant has already been set
forth above when we were reviewing Plutarch's "Instruction of
Trajan"; and the duties of the prince and of the different members of the commonwealth were also carefully explained at that
point. Wherefore it will be easier to make known here, and in
fewer words, the opposite characteristics of the tyrant. A tyrant,
then, as the philosophers have described him, is one who oppresses
the people by rulership based upon force, while he who rules in
accordance with the laws is a prince. Law is the gift of God,
the model of equity, a standard of justice, a likeness of the divine
will, the guardian of well-being, a bond of union and solidarity
between peoples, a rule defining duties, a barrier against the vices

SOURCE. "On Tyranny and Tyrannicide," in *The Statesman's Book of
John of Salisbury,* John Dickinson, tr., New York, Alfred A. Knopf, Inc.,
1927, pp. 335–336 and 372–373. Copyright by Alfred A. Knopf, Inc., 1927.
Copyright by Lindsay Rogers, 1955. Reprinted by permission of Appleton-
Century-Crofts.

and the destroyer thereof, a punishment of violence and all wrong-
doing. The law is assailed by force or by fraud, and, as it were,
either wrecked by the fury of the lion or undermined by the
wiles of the serpent. In whatever way this comes to pass, it is
plain that it is the grace of God which is being assailed, and that
it is God himself who in a sense is challenged to battle. The prince
fights for the laws and the liberty of the people; the tyrant thinks
nothing done unless he brings the laws to nought and reduces
the people to slavery. Hence the prince is a kind of likeness of
divinity; and the tyrant, on the contrary, a likeness of the boldness of the Adversary, even of the wickedness of Lucifer, imi-
tating him that sought to build his throne to the north and make
himself like unto the Most High, with the exception of His goodness. For had he desired to be like unto Him in goodness, he
would never have striven to tear from Him the glory of His
power and wisdom. What he more likely did aspire to was to
be equal with him in authority to dispense rewards. The prince,
as the likeness of the Deity, is to be loved, worshipped and cher-
ished; the tyrant, the likeness of wickedness, is generally to be
even killed. The origin of tyranny is iniquity, and springing from
a poisonous root, it is a tree which grows and sprouts into a bale-
ful pestilent growth, and to which the axe must by all means
be laid. For if iniquity and injustice, banishing charity, had not
brought about tyranny, firm concord and perpetual peace would
have possessed the peoples of the earth forever, and no one would
think of enlarging his boundaries. Then kingdoms would be as
friendly and peaceful, according to the authority of the great
father Augustine, and would enjoy as undisturbed repose, as the
separate families in a well-ordered state, or as different persons
in the same family; or perhaps, which is even more credible,
there would be no kingdoms at all, since it is clear from the
ancient historians that in the beginning these were founded by
iniquity as presumptuous encroachments against the Lord, or else
were extorted from Him. . . .

The histories teach, however, that none should undertake the
death of a tyrant who is bound to him by an oath or by the obligation of fealty. For we read that Sedechias, because he disre-
garded the sacred obligation of fealty, was led into captivity; and
that in the case of another of the kings of Juda whose name

escapes my memory, his eyes were plucked out because, falling into faithlessness, he did not keep before his sight God, to whom the oath is taken; since sureties for good behavior are justly given even to a tyrant.

But as for the use of poison, although I see it sometimes wrongfully adopted by infidels, I do not read that it is ever permitted by any law. Not that I do not believe that tyrants ought to be removed from our midst, but it should be done without loss of religion and honor. For David, the best of all kings that I have read of, and who, save in the incident of Urias Etheus, walked blamelessly in all things, although he had to endure the most grievous tyrant, and although he often had an opportunity of destroying him, yet preferred to spare him, trusting in the mercy of God, within whose power it was to set him free without sin. He therefore determined to abide in patience until the tyrant should either suffer a change of heart and be visited by God with return of charity, or else should fall in battle, or otherwise meet his end by the just judgment of God. How great was his patience can be discerned from the fact that when he had cut off the edge of Saul's robe in the cave, and again when, having entered the camp by night, he rebuked the negligence of the sentinels, in both cases he compelled the king to confess that David was acting the juster part. And surely the method of destroying tyrants which is the most useful and the safest, is for those who are oppressed to take refuge humbly in the protection of God's mercy, and lifting up undefiled hands to the Lord, to pray devoutly that the scourge wherewith they are afflicted may be turned aside from them. For the sins of transgressors are the strength of tyrants.

HUMANISM

7   *Frederick B. Artz*
      The Interests of the Humanists

*"Humanism" has often been taken as a key characteristic of the
Italian Renaissance, yet scholars have found strong elements of
humanism in the twelfth century. To complicate the problem, there
is considerable disagreement as to how the word should be defined.
Some would define "humanism" simply as a love and concern for
human beings. To others, it is a preoccupation with this world rather
than the next. To still others it is a devotion to the humanistic disciplines—the humanities—language, literature, and history in particular.
Finally, the word has often been associated with an interest in the
literary culture of Greco-Roman antiquity.*

*The most common scholarly definition of "humanism" would com-
bine all four of the preceding definitions. Emphasis would be placed
on the last two, with the understanding that the humanities in general,
and Classical culture in particular, were indeed concerned with
human beings and the corporeal world. Thus most scholars would
agree that humanism flourished in the Latin literary revival of the
later eleventh and twelfth centuries, but gave way in the thirteenth
century to a nonhumanistic emphasis on dialectic—that is, philosophical and theological rationalism. Such was the interpretation of Erwin
Panofsky in the passage quoted earlier in this book. Such is the interpretation of Frederick Artz in this excerpt. But in reading Artz, one*

SOURCE. Frederick B. Artz, "The Interests of the Humanists," in *The
Mind of the Middle Ages*, New York: Alfred A. Knopf, Inc., 1953, third
revised edition, 1958, pp. 432–435. Copyright 1953 by Alfred A. Knopf, Inc.,
Reprinted by permission of the author and the publisher.

should bear in mind that an articulate, scholarly minority would dissent from the proposition that the thirteenth-century scholastic philosophers were nonhumanistic. The scholastics may have neglected Latin belles lettres, but they were deeply concerned with human beings. Thus, according to the broadest definition of the word, they were humanists. As the modern Catholic philosopher Etienne Gilson has observed,

"*The difference between the Renaissance and the Middle Ages is not a difference of excess but of default. The Renaissance, as it is commonly described, is not the Middle Ages plus man, but the Middle Ages minus God, and the tragedy is that in losing God the Renaissance lost man himself. . . . Accordingly, if Humanism is considered in the fullness of its essence, and in its spirit no less than in its letter, then far from saying that it underwent a reversal in the thirteenth century, one should say that this was the century of its full embodiment.*" [*Les idées et les lettres (Paris, 1932), p. 192; tr. C. W. Hollister.*]

From this persuasive statement of the minority viewpoint, we turn now to Professor Artz' analysis, based on the more widely held definition of "humanism."

Mediaeval men were, as we have seen, the inheritors of a double antiquity; they were the heirs of Graeco-Roman culture as well as of the traditions of Judaism and early Christianity. They never lost contact with either tradition, though, after the fall of Rome, it was not until the eleventh and twelfth centuries that they began fully to understand and to use their inherited riches. So while the mystics and reformers were rediscovering the legacy of early Christianity, the humanists were entering more thoroughly into the cultural heritage which had been left to them by the great centuries of classical antiquity.

Humanism may be defined as an enthusiasm for the literature of Greece and Rome, both for its style and for its ideas. While in no mediaeval century had such enthusiasm been entirely quenched, it was stronger at times than at others. There had been a great revival of interest in the Latin classics in the schools of the Carolingian and Ottonian periods. The Barbarian raids of the tenth century had created chaos in many areas of western Europe, and not until the eleventh and twelfth centuries does another revival appear. This so-called "Renaissance of the Twelfth Century" was particularly marked in the cathedral schools of Chartres, Paris, and Orléans. Of these the School of Chartres . . . became the most famous. Here in the eleventh century, Fulbert, a pupil of Gerbert of Aurillac, had introduced an improved study of the seven liberal arts. The students spoke of Fulbert, their chief teacher, as "a venerable Socrates." The teaching at Chartres was very thorough though by no means revolutionary. In literary subjects, the chief authors studied were Cicero, Livy, Ovid, Horace, Virgil, and Statius, and the Christian classics of Augustine, Boethius, Fortunatus, and Bede, always with the aid of the grammarians, Donatus and Priscian. Evidently great attention was paid to teaching the students to write effective Latin prose and verse. The pupils we know were taught to write both verse with a stress rhythm and verse based on the ancient Roman system of quantity.

In the twelfth century, Bernard of Chartres, Thierry, and John of Salisbury raised the instruction at Chartres to a level beyond that of any other school in Latin Christendom. John of Salisbury describes the methods used by Bernard of Chartres:

"By citations from the authors, he brought into relief the grammatical figures, the rhetorical colors, the artifices of sophistry, and pointed out how the text in hand bore on other studies. He inculcated correctness of diction, and a fitting use of figures. Realizing that practice strengthens memory and sharpens faculty, he urged his pupils to imitate what they had heard. The evening exercise was filled with such an abundance of grammar that any one, by attending it for a year, would have at his fingers' end the art of writing and speaking. For those boys who had to write exercises in prose or verse, he selected the poets and orators, and showed how they should be imitated in the linking of words. Yet Bernard pointed out to awkward borrowers that whoever imitated the ancients should himself become worthy of imitation by posterity. He impressed upon his pupils the virtue of economy, and the values of words. He explained where a meagerness of diction was fitting, and where copiousness should be allowed, and the advantage of due measure everywhere. He admonished them to go through the histories and poems with diligence, and daily to fix passages in their memory."

The teaching at Chartres in the first half of the twelfth century probably differed in quality rather than in kind from what was taught in other schools. From a pupil of the cathedral school of Paris, where literary studies and a fine style in Latin verse and prose were also cultivated, came the famous grammar and rhetoric, the *Doctrinale*, of Alexander de Villedieu. The work is fuller and more systematic than that of Priscian, and it has the advantage of using the *Vulgate* and the Christian Latin writers as examples, and of conforming to contemporary usage. For the next three centuries it remained the common textbook for the teaching of grammar all over Latin Christendom. In Italy the schools also laid great emphasis on the art of writing, the *ars dictaminis*, though the purpose was sometimes only to teach pupils to write official letters and to draw up legal documents. In many Italian schools the study of grammar and rhetoric became hardly more than a short business course. The Italian *ars dictaminis* and *ars notaria* (for drafting legal documents) in the later twelfth and thirteenth centuries spread over France and other parts of western Europe.

The flowering of Latin literary studies centering in northern France in the first half of the twelfth century promised to lead to a great revival of classical literary studies. Students from these northern French cathedral schools taught all over western Europe, and some of them carried the gospel of the study of humane letters far and wide. That the humanism of the twelfth century was on the way to a real comprehension of classical civilization is shown in the writings of John of Salisbury. Very rarely does any reference of his to the ancient world startle the modern reader as fantastic or fabulous as do those of most mediaeval writers, including Dante. John shows also a just understanding of the character of many of the leading men of antiquity. The humanism of the twelfth century was a clerical humanism in opposition to the growth of ascetic idealism. It showed a new awareness of this world, and, through this awareness, it came to understand better the world of Greece and Rome. But this humanistic movement was cut short by the growing interest in dialectical and theological studies stimulated by the recovery of Greek and Arabic learning. Literary studies did not disappear, but they did not continue to fulfill the promise of the French cathedral schools of the earlier part of the twelfth century. Already by 1215 the classical authors are absent from the arts course in the University of Paris, and a curriculum of 1255 prescribes only Donatus and Priscian among Latin authors, and throws all its emphasis on the new versions of Aristotle. In the *Battle of the Seven Liberal Arts*, a poem of 1250, the dialecticians of Paris defeat the grammarians of Orléans. Literary form came to be despised, and logic professed to be able to supply any defects in a man's grammatical studies. By the later thirteenth century grammar had become a logical science.

What the "Renaissance of the Twelfth Century" had been on the verge of accomplishing was achieved by Italy in the fourteenth and fifteenth centuries. The Italian humanists came to be the heirs and successors of the mediaeval rhetoricians. These Italian humanists, however, did not invent a new field of learning nor did they create a new profession.

8   FROM   *William of Malmesbury*
The Deeds of the Kings of the English

William of Malmesbury, an English monk of the first half of the twelfth century, was one of the most distinguished historians of the High Middle Ages. Well-read in the literature of Roman Antiquity, he was by both training and profession a humanist, and his histories are laden with comparisons and parallels from the Classical historians.

In order to provide an insight into William of Malmesbury's historical methodology and approach, a number of the prefaces and

SOURCE. William of Malmesbury, *The Deeds of the Kings of the English*, J. A. Giles, tr., London: Henry G. Bohn, 1847, pp. 4, 93–94, 258–259, 325–326, 424; 276–278, 301–302.

prologues to various parts of his masterpiece, The Deeds of the Kings of the English, *are presented here in direct sequence. These introductory passages are followed by two illustrations of William's historical writing: (1) his description of the Battle of Hastings, 1066, and (2) one of his miracle stories. The miracle story illustrates the gap that exists between a perceptive historian of the twelfth century and a historian of Classical Antiquity or the Italian Renaissance.*

FROM THE PREFACE TO THE WORK

. . . "Should any one, however," to use the poet's expression, "peruse this work with sensible delight,"[1] I deem it necessary to acquaint him, that I vouch nothing for the truth of long past transactions, but the consonance of the time; the veracity of the relation must rest with its authors. Whatever I have recorded of later times, I have either myself seen, or heard from credible authority. However, in either part, I pay but little respect to the judgment of my contemporaries: trusting that I shall gain with posterity, when love and hatred shall be no more, if not a reputation for eloquence, at least credit for diligence.

BOOK II. PROLOGUE

A long period has elapsed since, as well through the care of my parents as my own industry, I became familiar with books. This pleasure possessed me from my childhood: this source of delight has grown with my years. Indeed I was so instructed by my father, that, had I turned aside to other pursuits, I should have considered it as jeopardy to my soul and discredit to my character. Wherefore mindful of the adage "covet what is necessary," I constrained my early age to desire eagerly that which it was disgraceful not to possess. I gave, indeed, my attention to various branches of literature, but in different degrees. Logic, for instance, which gives arms to eloquence, I contented myself

---

[1] From Virgil, Sixth Eclogue.

with barely hearing. Medicine, which ministers to the health of the body, I studied with somewhat more attention. But now, having scrupulously examined the several branches of Ethics, I bow down to its majesty, because it spontaneously unveils itself to those who study it, and directs their minds to moral practice; History more especially; which, by an agreeable recapitulation of past events, excites its readers, by example, to frame their lives to the pursuit of good, or to aversion from evil. When, therefore, at my own expense, I had procured some historians of foreign nations, I proceeded, during my domestic leisure, to inquire if any thing concerning our own country could be found worthy of handing down to posterity. Hence it arose, that, not content with the writings of ancient times, I began, myself, to compose; not indeed to display my learning, which is comparatively nothing,[2] but to bring to light events lying concealed in the confused mass of antiquity. In consequence rejecting vague opinions, I have studiously sought for chronicles far and near, though I confess I have scarcely profited any thing by this industry. For perusing them all, I still remained poor in information; though I ceased not my researches as long as I could find any thing to read. However, what I have clearly ascertained concerning the four kingdoms,[3] I have inserted in my first book, in which I hope truth will find no cause to blush, though perhaps a degree of doubt may sometimes arise. I shall now trace the monarchy of the West Saxon kingdom, through the line of successive princes, down to the coming of the Normans: which if any person will condescend to regard with complacency, let him in brotherly love observe the following rule: "If before, he knew only these things, let him not be disgusted because I have inserted them; if he shall know more, let him not be angry that I have not spoken of them"; but rather let him communicate his knowledge to me, while I yet live, that at least, those events may appear in the margin of my history, which do not occur in the text.

[2] This expression of modesty, characteristic of most medieval writers, contrasts sharply with the self-esteem of many of the writers of the Italian Renaissance.

[3] The four major kingdoms of Anglo-Saxon England at the time of the first Danish invasions (late eighth and ninth centuries): Wessex, Mercia, East Anglia, and Northumbria.

BOOK III. PREFACE

Normans and English, incited by different motives, have written of king William:[4] the former have praised him to excess; extolling to the utmost both his good and his bad actions: while the latter, out of national hatred, have laden their conqueror with undeserved reproach. For my part, as the blood of either people flows in my veins, I shall steer a middle course: where I am certified of his good deeds, I shall openly proclaim them; his bad conduct I shall touch upon lightly and sparingly, though not so as to conceal it; so that neither shall my narrative be condemned as false, nor will I brand that man with ignominious censure, almost the whole of whose actions may reasonably be excused, if not commended. Wherefore I shall willingly and carefully relate such anecdotes of him, as may be matter of incitement to the indolent, or of example to the enterprising; useful to the present age, and pleasing to posterity. But I shall spend little time in relating such things as are of service to no one, and which produce disgust in the reader, as well as ill-will to the author. There are always people, more than sufficient, ready to detract from the actions of the noble: my course of proceeding will be, to extenuate evil, as much as can be consistently with truth, and not to bestow excessive commendation even on good actions. For this moderation, as I imagine, all true judges will esteem me neither timid, nor unskilful. And this rule too, my history will regard equally, with respect both to William and his two sons; that nothing shall be dwelt on too fondly; nothing untrue shall be admitted. The elder of these[5] did little worthy of praise, if we except the early part of his reign; gaining, throughout the whole of his life, the favour of the military at the expense of the people. The second,[6] more obsequious to his father than to his brother, possessed his spirit, unsubdued either by prosperity or adversity: on regarding his warlike expeditions, it is matter of doubt, whether he was more cautious or more bold; on contemplating their event, whether he was more fortunate, or unsuccessful.

[4] William I, the Conquerer, 1066–1087.
[5] William II, "Rufus," 1087–1100.
[6] Henry I, 1100–1135.

There will be a time, however, when the reader may judge for himself. I am now about to begin my third volume; and I think I have said enough to make him attentive, and disposed to receive instruction: his own feelings will persuade him to be candid.

BOOK IV. PREFACE

I am aware, that many persons think it unwise in me, to have written the history of the kings of my own time; alleging, that in such a work, truth is often made shipwreck of, while falsehood meets with support: because to relate the crimes of contemporaries, is attended with danger; their good actions with applause. Whence it arises, say they, that, as all things have, now, a natural tendency to evil rather than to good, the historian passes over any disgraceful transaction, however obvious, through timidity; and, for the sake of approbation, feigns good qualities, when he cannot find them. There are others, who, judging of us by their own indolence, deem us unequal to so great a task, and brand our undertaking with malignant censure. Wherefore, impelled by the reasoning of the one, or the contempt of the other, I had long since voluntarily retired to leisure and to silence: but, after indulging in them for a time, the accustomed inclination for study again strongly beset me; as it was impossible for me to be unoccupied, and I knew not how to give myself up to those forensic avocations, which are beneath the notice of a literary character. To this was to be added the incitements of my friends, to whose suggestions, though only implied, I ought to pay regard: and they indeed gently urged me, already sufficiently disposed, to prosecute my undertaking. Animated, therefore, by the advice of those whom I love most affectionately, I advance to give them a lasting pledge of friendship from the stores of my research. Grateful also to those who are in fear for me, lest I should either excite hatred, or disguise the truth, I will, by the help of Christ, make such a return for their kindness, as neither to become odious, nor a falsifier. For I will describe, both what has been done well, or otherwise, in such wise, and so safely steer between Scylla and Charybdis, that my opinions shall not be concealed, though some matters may be omitted in my history. Moreover, to those who undervalue the labours of others, I make the same answer as St. Jerome formerly did to his critics; "Let them read if they like: if not, let them cast it aside; because I do not obtrude my work on the fastidious, but I dedicate it, if any think it worth their notice, to the studious"; which even these men will readily pronounce to be consonant to equity, unless they are of the number of those, of whom it is said; "Fools are easy to confute, but not so easy to restrain." I will relate, then, in this, the fourth book of my work, every thing which may be said of William, son of William the Great,[7] in such manner that neither shall the truth suffer, nor shall the dignity of the prince be obscured. Some matters also will be inserted in these pages, which in his time were calamitous in this country, or glorious elsewhere, as far as my knowledge extends. More especially, the pilgrimage of the Christians to Jerusalem, which it will be proper to annex in this place;[8] because an expedition, so famous in these times, is well worth hearing, and will also be an incitement to valour. Not indeed that I have any confidence these transactions will be better treated by me than by others who have written on the subject, but that, what many write, many may read. Yet, lest so long a preface should disgust my reader, I will immediately enter on my work.

BOOK V. PREFACE

Summoned by the progress of events, we have entered on the times of king Henry;[9] to transmit whose actions to posterity, requires an abler hand than ours. For, were only those particulars recorded which have reached our knowledge, they would weary the most eloquent, and might overload a library. Who, then, will attempt to unfold in detail all his profound counsels, all his royal achievements? These are matters too deep for me, and

---

[7] Again the reference is to King William Rufus (1087–1100), son of William the Conqueror.

[8] The First Crusade (1096–1099).

[9] Again, Henry I (1100–1135), youngest son of William the Conqueror and a contemporary of William of Malmesbury. The latter dedicated his work to Henry I's natural son, Earl Robert of Gloucester, a fact which might explain in part William of Malmesbury's enthusiasm for Henry I.

require more leisure than I possess. Scarcely Cicero himself, whose eloquence is venerated by all the Western world, would attempt it in prose; and in verse, not even a rival of the Mantuan Bard. In addition to this, it is to be observed, that while I, who am a man of retired habits, and far from the secrets of a court, withhold my assent from doubtful relators, being ignorant of his greater achievements, I touch only on a few events. Wherefore, it is to be feared, that where my information falls beneath my wishes, the hero, whose numerous exploits I omit, may appear to suffer. However, for this, if it be a fault, I shall have a good excuse with him who shall recollect that I could not be acquainted with the whole of his transactions, nor ought I to relate even all that I did know. The insignificance of my condition effects the one; the disgust of my readers would be excited by the other. This fifth book, then, will display some few of his deeds, while fame, no doubt, will blazon the rest, and lasting memory transmit them to posterity. Nor will it deviate from the design of the preceding four, but particularise some things which happened during his time here and elsewhere, which perchance are either unrecorded, or unknown to many: they will occupy, indeed, a considerable portion of the volume, while I must claim the usual indulgence for long digressions, as well in this as in the others.

THE BATTLE OF HASTINGS, 1066

The courageous leaders mutually prepared for battle, each according to his national custom. The English, as we have heard, passed the night without sleep, in drinking and singing, and, in the morning, proceeded without delay towards the enemy; all were on foot, armed with battle-axes, and covering themselves in front by the junction of their shields, they formed an impenetrable body, which would have secured their safety that day, had not the Normans, by a feigned flight, induced them to open their ranks, which till that time, according to their custom, were closely compacted. The king himself on foot, stood, with his brother, near the standard; in order that, while all shared equal danger, none might think of retreating. This standard William

sent, after the victory, to the pope; it was sumptuously em-
broidered, with gold and precious stones, in the form of a man
fighting.

On the other side, the Normans passed the whole night in
confessing their sins, and received the sacrament in the morning:
their infantry, with bows and arrows, formed the vanguard,
while their cavalry, divided into wings, were thrown back. The
earl,[10] with serene countenance, declaring aloud, that God would
favour his, as being the righteous side, called for his arms; and
presently, when, through the hurry of his attendants, he had
put on his hauberk the hind part before, he corrected the mistake
with a laugh; saying, "My dukedom shall be turned into a kingdom." Then beginning the song of Roland, that the warlike example of that man might stimulate the soldiers, and calling on
God for assistance, the battle commenced on both sides. They
fought with ardour, neither giving ground, for great part of the
day. Finding this, William gave a signal to his party, that, by
a feigned flight, they should retreat. Through this device, the
close body of the English, opening for the purpose of cutting
down the straggling enemy, brought upon itself swift destruc-
tion; for the Normans, facing about, attacked them thus dis-
ordered, and compelled them to fly. In this manner, deceived
by a stratagem, they met an honourable death in avenging their
country; nor indeed were they at all wanting to their own revenge, as, by frequently making a stand, they slaughtered their
pursuers in heaps: for, getting possession of an eminence, they
drove down the Normans, when roused with indignation and
anxiously striving to gain the higher ground, into the valley
beneath, where, easily hurling their javelins and rolling down
stones on them as they stood below, they destroyed them to a
man. Besides, by a short passage, with which they were acquainted, avoiding a deep ditch, they trod under foot such a
multitude of their enemies in that place, that they made the hol-
low level with the plain, by the heaps of carcasses. This vicissi-
tude of first one party conquering, and then the other, prevailed
as long as the life of Harold[11] continued; but when he fell, from

[10] Duke William of Normandy: William the Conqueror.
[11] Harold Godwinson, King of England (January-October, 1066).

having his brain pierced with an arrow, the flight of the English ceased not until night. The valour of both leaders was here eminently conspicuous.

Harold, not merely content with the duty of a general in exhorting others, diligently entered into every soldier-like office; often would he strike the enemy when coming to close quarters, so that none could approach him with impunity; for immediately the same blow levelled both horse and rider. Wherefore, as I have related, receiving the fatal arrow from a distance, he yielded to death. One of the soldiers with a sword gashed his thigh, as he lay prostrate; for which shameful and cowardly action, he was branded with ignomy by William, and dismissed from service.

William too was equally ready to encourage by his voice and by his presence; to be the first to rush forward; to attack the thickest of the foe. Thus everywhere raging, everywhere furious, he lost three choice horses, which were that day pierced under him. The dauntless spirit and vigor of the intrepid general, however, still persisted, though often called back by the kind remonstrance of his body-guard; he still persisted, I say, till approaching night crowned him with complete victory. And no doubt, the hand of God so protected him, that the enemy should draw no blood from his person, though they aimed so many javelins at him.

ARCHBISHOP MAURILIUS OF ROUEN RETURNS FROM THE DEAD

To Malger succeeded Maurilius of Feschamp;[12] a monk commendable for many virtues, but principally for his abstinence. After a holy and well-spent life, when he came, by the call of God, to his end, bereft of vital breath, he lay, as it were, dead for almost half a day. Nevertheless, when preparation was made to carry him into the church, recovering his breath, he bathed the by-standers in tears of joy, and comforted them, when lost in amazement, with this address: "Let your minds be attentive while you hear the last words of your pastor. I have died a nat-

[12] As archbishop of Rouen.

ural death, but I am come back, to relate to you what I have seen; yet shall I not continue with you long, because it delights me to sleep in the Lord. The conductors of my spirit were adorned with every elegance both of countenance and attire; the gentleness of their speech accorded with the splendour of their garments; so much so, that I could wish for nothing more than the attentions of such men. Delighted therefore with their soothing approbation, I went, as it appeared to me, towards the east. A seat in paradise was promised me, which I was shortly to enter. In a moment, passing over Europe and entering Asia, we came to Jerusalem; where, having worshipped the saints, we proceeded to Jordan. The residents on the hither bank joining company with my conductors, made a joyful party. I was now hastening to pass over the river, through longing desire to see what was beyond it, when my companions informed me, that God had commanded, that I must first be terrified by the sight of the demons; in order that the venial sins, which I had not wiped out by confession, might be expiated, by the dread of terrific forms. As soon as this was said, there came opposite to me, such a multitude of devils, brandishing pointed weapons, and breathing out fire, that the plain appeared like steel, and the air like flame. I was so dreadfully alarmed at them, that had the earth clave asunder, or the heaven opened, I should not have known whither to have betaken myself for safety. Thus panic-struck, and doubting whither to go, I suddenly recovered my life, though instantaneously about to lose it again, that by this relation I might be serviceable to your salvation, unless you neglect it:" and almost as soon as he had so said, he breathed out his soul. His body, then buried under ground, in the church of St. Mary, is now, by divine miracle, as they report, raised up more than three feet above the earth.

LITERATURE AND LOVE

9   *C. S. Lewis*
The Allegory of Love

The "Twelfth-Century Renaissance" witnessed the genesis of a tradition of romantic love that began in southern France, spread northward during the second half of the twelfth century, and affected the style of masculine-feminine relationships down to the present day. The effects of the medieval courtly love tradition on literature and social history have been immense. The tradition underlay the lyric poetry of eleventh- and twelfth-century Languedoc and the romance literature of twelfth- and thirteenth-century northern Europe: Tristan and Iseult, the Arthurian tales, *and many similar works. Thus the tradition is exceedingly important in itself. Its relevance to the more technical aspects of the Renaissance debate lies in the question of self-awareness. To the argument that the Italian Renaissance marked the first stage of the self-discovery of Western man, it may be replied that the lovers and romantic writers of the High Middle Ages exhibited a great degree—often an agonizing degree—of self-awareness.*

The subject of courtly love is introduced by an excerpt from The Allegory of Love *by the English scholar, novelist, and Christian apologist, C. S. Lewis.*

Every one has heard of courtly love, and every one knows that it appears quite suddenly at the end of the eleventh century in

SOURCE. C. S. Lewis, *The Allegory of Love*, London: Oxford University Press, 1936, pp. 2–5. Copyright 1936 by Oxford University Press. Reprinted by permission of the Clarendon Press, Oxford.

Languedoc. The characteristics of the Troubadour poetry have been repeatedly described. With the form, which is lyrical, and the style, which is sophisticated and often "aureate" or deliberately enigmatic, we need not concern ourselves. The sentiment, of course, is love, but love of a highly specialized sort, whose characteristics may be enumerated as Humility, Courtesy, Adultery, and the Religion of Love. The lover is always abject. Obedience to his lady's lightest wish, however whimsical, and silent acquiescence in her rebukes, however unjust, are the only virtues he dares to claim. There is a service of love closely modelled on the service which a feudal vassal owes to his lord. The lover is the lady's "man." He addresses her as *midons*, which etymologically represents not "my lady" but "my lord." The whole attitude has been rightly described as "a feudalisation of love." This solemn amatory ritual is felt to be part and parcel of the courtly life. It is possible only to those who are, in the old sense of the word, polite. It thus becomes, from one point of view the flower, from another the seed, of all those noble usages which distinguish the gentle from the vilein: only the courteous can love, but it is love that makes them courteous. Yet this love, though neither playful nor licentious in its expression, is always what the nineteenth century called "dishonourable" love. The poet normally addresses another man's wife, and the situation is so carelessly accepted that he seldom concerns himself much with her husband: his real enemy is the rival. But if he is ethically careless, he is no light-hearted gallant: his love is represented as a despairing and tragical emotion—or almost despairing, for he is saved from complete wanhope by his faith in the God of Love who never betrays his faithful worshippers and who can subjugate the cruelest beauties.

The characteristics of this sentiment, and its systematic coherence throughout the love poetry of the Troubadours as a whole, are so striking that they easily lead to a fatal misunderstanding. We are tempted to treat "courtly love" as a mere episode in literary history—an episode that we have finished with as we have finished with the peculiarities of Skaldic verse or Euphuistic prose. In fact, however, an unmistakable continuity connects the Provençal love song with the love poetry of the later Middle Ages, and thence, through Petrarch and many others,

with that of the present day. If the thing at first escapes our
notice, this is because we are so familiar with the erotic tradition
of modern Europe that we mistake it for something natural and
universal and therefore do not inquire into its origins. It seems
to us natural that love should be the commonest theme of serious
imaginative literature: but a glance at classical antiquity or at
the Dark Ages at once shows us that what we took for "nature"
is really a special state of affairs, which will probably have an
end, and which certainly had a beginning in eleventh-century
Provence. It seems—or it seemed to us till lately—a natural thing
that love (under certain conditions) should be regarded as a noble
and ennobling passion: it is only if we imagine ourselves trying
to explain this doctrine to Aristotle, Virgil, St. Paul, or the author
of *Beowulf*, that we become aware how far from natural it is.
Even our code of etiquette, with its rule that women always have
precedence, is a legacy from courtly love, and is felt to be far
from natural in modern Japan or India. Many of the features of
this sentiment, as it was known to the Troubadours, have indeed
disappeared; but this must not blind us to the fact that the most
momentous and the most revolutionary elements in it have made
the background of European literature for eight hundred years.
French poets, in the eleventh century, discovered or invented,
or were the first to express, that romantic species of passion which
English poets were still writing about in the nineteenth. They
effected a change which has left no corner of our ethics, our
imagination, of our daily life untouched, and they erected impass-
able barriers between us and the classical past or the Oriental
present. Compared with this revolution the Renaissance is a mere
ripple on the surface of literature.

There can be no mistake about the novelty of romantic love:
our only difficulty is to imagine in all its bareness the mental
world that existed before its coming—to wipe out of our minds,
for a moment, nearly all that makes the food both of modern
sentimentality and modern cynicism. We must conceive a world
emptied of that ideal of "happiness"—a happiness grounded on
successful romantic love—which still supplies the motive of our
popular fiction. In ancient literature love seldom rises above the
levels of merry sensuality or domestic comfort, except to be

treated as a tragic madness, an ατη which plunges otherwise sane
people (usually women) into crime and disgrace. Such is the
love of Medea, of Phaedra, of Dido; and such the love from
which maidens pray that the gods may protect them. At the other
end of the scale we find the comfort and utility of a good wife
acknowledged: Odysseus loves Penelope as he loves the rest of
his home and possessions, and Aristotle rather grudgingly admits
that the conjugal relation may now and then rise to the same level
as the virtuous friendship between good men. But this has plainly
very little to do with "love" in the modern or medieval sense; and
if we turn to ancient love-poetry proper, we shall be even more
disappointed. We shall find the poets loud in their praises of love,
no doubt. . . . "What is life without love, tra-la-la?" as the later
song has it. But this is no more to be taken seriously than the
countless panegyrics both ancient and modern on the all-consoling
virtues of the bottle. If Catullus and Propertius vary the strain
with cries of rage and misery, this is not so much because they
are romantics as because they are exhibitionists. In their anger
or their suffering they care not who knows the pass to which love
has brought them. They are in the grip of the ατη. They do not
expect their obsession to be regarded as a noble sorrow—they
have no "silks and fine array."

Plato will not be reckoned an exception by those who have
read him with care. In the *Symposium*, no doubt, we find the
conception of a ladder whereby the soul may ascend from human
love to divine. But this is a ladder in the strictest sense; you reach
the higher rungs by leaving the lower ones behind. The original
object of human love—who, incidentally, is not a woman has
simply fallen out of sight before the soul arrives at the spiritual
object. The very first step upwards would have made a courtly
lover blush, since it consists in passing on from the worship of
the beloved's beauty to that of the same beauty in others. Those
who call themselves Platonists at the Renaissance may imagine a
love which reaches the divine without abandoning the human
and becomes spiritual while remaining also carnal; but they do
not find this in Plato. If they read it into him, this is because they
are living, like ourselves, in the tradition which began in the
eleventh century.

10   *Beatritz de Dia*
               I Live in Grave Anxiety

   Beatritz de Dia, a lyric poetess of mid-twelfth-century Languedoc, is somewhat exceptional in that she expresses emotions customarily voiced by male troubadours. But her lyric poem "I Live in Grave Anxiety" is characteristic of the medieval southern French lyric tradition.

I live in grave anxiety
For one fair knight who loved me so.
It would have made him glad to know
I loved him too—but silently.
I was mistaken, now I'm sure,
When I withheld myself from him.
My grief is deep, my days are dim,
And life itself has no allure.

I wish my knight might sleep with me
And hold me naked to his breast,
On my own form to take his rest,
And grieve no more, but joyous be.
My love for him surpasses all
The loves that famous lovers knew.
My soul is his, my body, too,
My heart, my life, are at his call.

My most beloved, dearest friend,
When will you fall into my power?
That I might lie with you an hour,
And love you 'til my life should end!
My heart is filled with passion's fire.
My well-loved knight, I grant thee grace,
To hold me in my husband's place,
And do the things I so desire.

SOURCE, C. Warren Hollister, tr. Copyright 1967 by John Wiley and Sons.

11 FROM   *Peter Abelard*
The Story of My Misfortunes

In this text we pass from the literature of love to love itself—to the most celebrated love affair of twelfth-century Europe. The love of Abelard and Héloïse was a fusion of intellects and emotions. Abelard possessed as keen a mind as any philosopher of his century and was the most famous logician of his day. Héloïse, who without Abelard would have been unknown to history, was nevertheless a woman of remarkable intellectual power. Both, too, were emotionally sensitive and artistically gifted. Abelard was a writer of love songs as well as philosophical treatises, and Héloïse has given us some of the most beautiful and searching love letters known to history. At the time of the lovers' first meeting Abelard was about thirty-seven years old, and Héloïse was seventeen.

And so, after a few days, I returned to Paris, and there for several years I peacefully directed the school which formerly had been destined for me, nay, even offered to me, but from which I had been driven out. At the very outset of my work there, I set about completing the glosses on Ezekiel which I had begun at Laon. These proved so satisfactory to all who read them that they came to believe me no less adept in lecturing on theology than I had proved myself to be in the field of philosophy. Thus my school was notably increased in size by reason of my lectures on subjects of both these kinds, and the amount of financial profit as well as glory which it brought to me cannot be concealed from you, for the matter was widely talked of. But prosperity always puffs up the foolish, and worldly comfort enervates the soul, rendering it an easy prey to carnal temptations. Thus I, who by this time had come to regard myself as the only philosopher remaining in

SOURCE. Peter Abelard, *The Story of My Misfortunes*, H. A. Bellows, tr., Glencoe: The Free Press, 1958, pp. 14–22 and 29–30. Copyright 1922. Reprinted by permission of The Free Press, a Division of The Macmillan Company.

the whole world, and had ceased to fear any further disturbance of my peace, began to loosen the rein on my desires, although hitherto I had always lived in the utmost continence. And the greater progress I made in my lecturing on philosophy or theology, the more I departed alike from the practice of the philosophers and the spirit of the divines in the uncleanness of my life. For it is well known, methinks, that philosophers, and still more those who have devoted their lives to arousing the love of sacred study, have been strong above all else in the beauty of chastity.

Thus did it come to pass that while I was utterly absorbed in pride and sensuality, divine grace, the cure for both diseases, was forced upon me, even though I, forsooth, would fain have shunned it. First was I punished for my sensuality, and then for my pride. For my sensuality I lost those things whereby I practiced it; for my pride, engendered in me by my knowledge of letters—and it is even as the Apostle said: "Knowledge puffeth itself up" (I Cor. viii, 1)—I knew the humiliation of seeing burned the very book in which I most gloried. And now it is my desire that you should know the stories of these two happenings, understanding them more truly from learning the very facts than from hearing what is spoken of them, and in the order in which they came about. Because I had ever held in abhorrence the foulness of prostitutes, because I had diligently kept myself from all excesses and from association with the women of noble birth who attended the school, because I knew so little of the common talk of ordinary people, perverse and subtly flattering chance gave birth to an occasion for casting me lightly down from the heights of my own exaltation. Nay, in such case not even divine goodness could redeem one who, having been so proud, was brought to such shame, were it not for the blessed gift of grace.

Now there dwelt in that same city of Paris a certain young girl named Héloïse, the niece of a canon who was called Fulbert. Her uncle's love for her was equalled only by his desire that she should have the best education which he could possibly procure for her. Of no mean beauty, she stood out above all by reason of her abundant knowledge of letters. Now this virtue is rare among women, and for that very reason it doubly graced the maiden, and made her the most worthy of renown in the entire kingdom. It was this young girl whom I, after carefully considering all those qualities which are wont to attract lovers, determined to unite with myself in the bonds of love, and indeed the thing seemed to me very easy to be done. So distinguished was my name, and I possessed the advantages of youth and comeliness, that no matter what woman I might favour with my love, I dreaded rejection of none. Then, too, I believed that I could win the maiden's consent all the more easily by reason of her knowledge of letters and her zeal therefor; so, even if we were parted, we might yet be together in thought with the aid of written messages. Perchance, too, we might be able to write more boldly than we could speak, and thus at all times could we live in joyous intimacy.

Thus, utterly aflame with my passion for this maiden, I sought to discover means whereby I might have daily and familiar speech with her, thereby the more easily to win her consent. For this purpose I persuaded the girl's uncle, with the aid of some of his friends, to take me into his household—for he dwelt hard by my school—in return for the payment of a small sum. My pretext for this was that the care of my own household was a serious handicap to my studies, and likewise burdened me with an expense far greater than I could afford. Now, he was a man keen in avarice, and likewise he was most desirous for his niece that her study of letters should ever go forward, so, for these two reasons, I easily won his consent to the fulfillment of my wish, for he was fairly agape for my money, and at the same time believed that his niece would vastly benefit by my teaching. More even than this, by his own earnest entreaties he fell in with my desires beyond anything I had dared to hope, opening the way for my love; for he entrusted her wholly to my guidance, begging me to give her instruction whensoever I might be free from the duties of my school, no matter whether by day or by night, and to punish her sternly if ever I should find her negligent of her tasks. In all this the man's simplicity was nothing short of astounding to me; I should not have been more smitten with wonder if he had entrusted a tender lamb to the care of a ravenous wolf. When he had thus given her into my charge, not alone to be taught but even to be disciplined, what had he done save to give free scope to my desires, and to offer me every opportunity, even if I had not sought it, to bend her to my will with threats and blows if I failed to do so with caresses? There were, however, two things

which particularly served to allay any foul suspicion: his own
love for his niece, and my former reputation for continence.

Why should I say more? We were united first in the dwelling
that sheltered our love, and then in the hearts that burned with it.
Under the pretext of study we spent our hours in the happiness
of love, and learning held out to us the secret opportunities that
our passion craved. Our speech was more of love than of the
books which lay open before us; our kisses far outnumbered our
reasoned words. Our hands sought less the book than each other's
bosoms; love drew our eyes together far more than the lesson
drew them to the pages of our text. In order that there might be
no suspicion, there were, indeed, sometimes blows, but love gave
them, not anger; they were the marks, not of wrath, but of a
tenderness surpassing the most fragrant balm in sweetness. What
followed? No degree in love's progress was left untried by our
passion, and if love itself could imagine any wonder as yet unknown, we discovered it. And our inexperience of such delights
made us all the more ardent in our pursuit of them, so that our
thirst for one another was still unquenched.

In measure as this passionate rapture absorbed me more and
more, I devoted ever less time to philosophy and to the work of
the school. Indeed, it became loathsome to me to go to the school
or to linger there; the labour, moreover was very burdensome,
since my nights were vigils of love and my days of study. My
lecturing became utterly careless and lukewarm; I did nothing
because of inspiration, but everything merely as a matter of habit.
I had become nothing more than a reciter of my former discoveries, and though I still wrote poems, they dealt with love,
not with the secrets of philosophy. Of these songs you yourself
well know how some have become widely known and have been
sung in many lands, chiefly, methinks, by those who delighted in
the things of this world. As for the sorrow, the groans, the lamen-
tations of my students when they perceived the preoccupation,
nay, rather the chaos, of my mind, it is hard even to imagine them.

A thing so manifest could deceive only a few, no one, methinks,
save him whose shame it chiefly bespoke, the girl's uncle, Fulbert.
The truth was often enough hinted to him, and by many persons,
but he could not believe it, partly, as I have said, by reason of his
boundless love for his niece, and partly because of the well-known

continence of my previous life. Indeed we do not easily suspect shame in those whom we most cherish, nor can there be the blot of foul suspicion on devoted love. Of this St. Jerome in his epistle to Sabinianus (Epist. 48) says: "We are wont to be the last to know the evils of our own households, and to be ignorant of the sins of our children and our wives, though our neighbours sing them aloud." But no matter how slow a matter may be in disclosing itself, it is sure to come forth at last, nor is it easy to hide from one what is known to all. So, after the lapse of several months, did it happen with us. Oh, how great was the uncle's grief when he learned the truth, and how bitter was the sorrow of the lovers when we were forced to part! With what shame was I overwhelmed, with what contrition smitten because of the blow which had fallen on her I loved, and what a tempest of misery burst over her by reason of my disgrace! Each grieved most, not for himself, but for the other. Each sought to allay, not his own sufferings, but those of the one he loved. The very sundering of our bodies served but to link our souls closer together; the plenitude of the love which was denied to us inflamed us more than ever. Once the wildness of shame had passed, it left us more shameless than before, as shame died within us the cause of it seemed to us ever more desirable. And so it chanced with us, as in the stories that the poets tell, it once happened with Mars and Venus when they were caught together.

It was not long after this that Héloïse found that she was pregnant, and of this she wrote to me in the utmost exaltation, at the same time asking me to consider what had best be done. Accordingly, on a night when her uncle was absent, we carried out the plan we had determined on, and I stole her secretly away from her uncle's house, sending her without delay to my own country. She remained there with my sister until she gave birth to a son, whom she named Astrolabe. Meanwhile her uncle, after his return, was almost mad with grief; only one who had then seen him could rightly guess the burning agony of his sorrow and the bitterness of his shame. What steps to take against me, or what snares to set for me, he did not know. If he should kill me or do me some bodily hurt, he feared greatly lest his dear-loved niece should be made to suffer for it among my kinsfolk. He had no power to seize me and imprison me somewhere against my will, though I make no doubt he would have done so quickly enough had he been able or dared, for I had taken measures to guard against any such attempt.

At length, however, in pity for his boundless grief, and bitterly blaming myself for the suffering which my love had brought upon him through the baseness of the deception I had practiced, I went to him to entreat his forgiveness, promising to make any amends that he himself might decree. I pointed out that what had happened could not seem incredible to any one who had ever felt the power of love, or who remembered how, from the very beginning of the human race, women had cast down even the noblest men to utter ruin. And in order to make amends even beyond his extremest hope, I offered to marry her whom I had seduced, provided only the thing could be kept secret, so that I might suffer no loss of reputation thereby. To this he gladly assented, pledging his own faith and that of his kindred, and sealing with kisses the pact which I had sought of him—and all this that he might the more easily betray me.

. . . After our little son was born, we left him in my sister's care, and secretly returned to Paris. A few days later, in the early morning, having kept our nocturnal vigil of prayer unknown to all in a certain church, we were united there in the benediction of wedlock, her uncle and a few friends of his and mine being present. We departed forthwith stealthily and by separate ways, nor thereafter did we see each other save rarely and in private, thus striving our utmost to conceal what we had done. But her uncle and those of his household, seeking solace for their disgrace, began to divulge the story of our marriage, and thereby to violate the pledge they had given me on this point. Héloïse, on the contrary, denounced her own kin and swore that they were speaking the most absolute lies. Her uncle, aroused to fury thereby, visited her repeatedly with punishments. No sooner had I learned this than I sent her to a convent of nuns at Argenteuil, not far from Paris, where she herself had been brought up and educated as a young girl. I had them make ready for her all the garments of a nun, suitable for the life of a convent, excepting only the veil, and these I bade her put on.

When her uncle and his kinsmen heard of this, they were convinced that now I had completely played them false and had rid myself forever of Héloïse by forcing her to become a nun. Violently incensed, they laid a plot against me, and one night, while I, all unsuspecting, was asleep in a secret room in my lodg ings, they broke in with the help of one of my servants, whom they had bribed. There they had vengeance on me with a most cruel and most shameful punishment, such as astounded the whole world, for they cut off those parts of my body with which I had done that which was the cause of their sorrow. This done, straightway they fled, but two of them were captured, and suffered the loss of their eyes and their genital organs. One of these two was the aforesaid servant, who, even while he was still in my service, had been led by his avarice to betray me.

12 *Héloïse*

Two Letters to Abelard

The two letters included here, composed by Héloïse in Latin, were written about twenty years after the first meeting of the lovers. Although married, they had long been apart and out of communication with one another. Héloïse, now about thirty-seven, is abbess of a convent, and Abelard is an abbot. The "letter to a friend" to which Héloïse alludes is, in fact, the autobiography—The Story of My Misfortunes—from which the preceding passages were taken. Abelard wrote his autobiography in the form of a letter to a friend, and its accidental passage into Héloïse's hands prompted her to write the first of the foregoing letters. Abelard replied, telling her of his difficulties relating to official condemnations of his philosophical doctrines. His letter was friendly but reserved and severely unromantic. He replied similarly to Héloïse's second letter, and, catching the hint, Héloïse took pains to keep her further correspondence with Abelard appropriately spiritual and antiseptic. Their relationship continued long thereafter, through letters, on a level of nonromantic friendship, with Abelard assuming the role of Héloïse's spiritual adviser. For Héloïse, evidently, these crumbs were far better than nothing at all.

SOURCE. Translated for this book by C. Warren Hollister.

FIRST LETTER TO ABELARD

Your letter, my beloved, written to a friend, chanced to reach me not long ago. Seeing from whom it was by its opening lines I burned to read it, because of my love for the writer, hoping too to recreate from its words an image of the man whose life I have ruined. Those words dropped gall and absinthe as they recalled to me the unhappy story of our relationship and the crosses you have ceaselessly borne, O my only one. Truly the letter must have convinced the friend that his troubles were slight compared to yours, as you showed the treachery and persecutions that followed you, the lies of your enemies and the burning of your glorious book, the connivings of false friends and the contemptible acts of those worthless monks whom you call your sons. Nobody could read it without tears. Your perils have reawakened my sorrows. All of us here despair of your life, and every day, with trembling hearts, we expect to hear the news of your death. In the name of Christ—who somehow has preserved you so far—inform us, His weak servants and yours—tell us with frequent letters of the storms that are overwhelming the swimmer, so that we, who alone remain yours, may share your pain or your joy. For one who grieves may be consoled by those who grieve with him; a burden borne by many is borne more lightly. And if this storm calms, how happy we will be to know it! Whatever your letters contain, they will show at least that we are not forgotten. Did not Seneca say in his letter to Lucilius that the letters of an absent friend are sweet? When malice cannot prevent your giving us this much of yourself, do not let neglect prove a hindrance.

You wrote that long letter to console a friend with the story of your own misfortunes, and in doing so you aroused our grief and increased our desolation. Heal these new wounds. You owe a deeper debt of friendship to us than to him, for we are not only friends but the dearest of friends—and your daughters. After God, you alone are the founder of this house, the creator of this oratory and this congregation. This new holy establishment is your own, and its delicate flowers need frequent watering. One who gives so much to his enemies should think of his own daugh-

ters. Or, forgetting for a moment the others that are here, consider how you owe this thing to me. What you owe to all women
under religious vows you should render all the more devotedly
to your only one. How many books the holy fathers have written
for the exhortation and instruction of holy women! I wonder at
your forgetfulness of these fragile beginnings of our conversation.
Neither respect for God nor love of us nor the example of the
blessed fathers has prompted you, either by speech or by letter,
to console me, adrift and consumed with sorrow. This duty was
all the stronger because the sacrament of marriage joined you
to me, and I—everybody sees it—cling to you with infinite love.

You know, dearest one—who does not know?—how much I
lost in you, and that an infamous act of treachery robbed me of
you and of myself at once. The greater my sorrow, the greater
my need for consolation, not from another but from you, so that
you who are alone the source of my sorrow may be alone my
consolation. It is you alone who can sadden me or gladden me
or bring me comfort. And you alone owe me this, especially
since I have obeyed your will so completely that, unable to offend
you, I suffered to ruin myself at your command. No, more than
that, love became madness and cut itself off from the hope of
that which alone it sought, when I obediently changed my garb,
and my heart too, so that I might prove you the sole owner of
my body as well as my spirit. God knows, I have always sought
in you only yourself, desiring only you and never what was
yours. I asked for no marriage bond, I sought no dowry. I have
tried to achieve not my own pleasure or will, but yours. And
if the name of wife seemed holier or mightier, the word mistress
was always sweeter to me, or even (do not be angry!) concubine
or harlot. For the more I lowered myself before you, the more
I hoped to win your favor and the less I should hinder the glory
of your fame. This you graciously remembered when con-
descending to point out in that letter to a friend some of the
reasons (but not all!) why I preferred love to marriage and
freedom to a chain.[1] As God is my witness, if Augustus, master
of the world, were to honor me with marriage and invest me

[1] The passage in Abelard's autobiography in which he tells of Héloïse's
arguments against their getting married was omitted from this volume.

with equal rule, it would still seem dearer and more honorable to me to be called your concubine than his empress. One who is rich and powerful is not the better man. That is a matter of fortune, this of merit. And a woman is avaricious who marries a rich man rather than a poor one and longs for a husband's wealth rather than for the husband himself. Such a woman deserves wages, not affection. She is seeking not the man but his property and would wish, if possible, to sell herself to one still wealthier. Aspasia expressed this clearly when she was trying to reconcile Xenophon with his wife: "Until you conclude that there is nowhere else a better man or more desirable woman, you will always be seeking someone whom you consider the best, and you will want to be married to the man or woman who is best of all." Truly this is a holy sentiment rather than a philosophical one, and wisdom speaks, not philosophy. This is the holy falsehood and blessed deception between man and wife when perfect and unimpaired affection keeps marriage inviolate, not so much by bodily innocence as by purity of mind. But what with other women is deception is in my case the clear truth, since what they imagine to be in their husbands, I—and the entire world agrees— know to be in you. My love for you is founded on truth and free of all error. Who among kings and philosophers can rival your fame? What land, what city does not thirst to see you? Who, I ask, has not rushed to behold you appearing in public, and craned his neck for a last glimpse as you left? What wife, what maiden has not longed for you when you were away and burned when you were present? What queen did not envy me my joys and my bed of love? You had two qualities by which you could win the soul of any woman: the gift of poetry and the gift of singing—gifts which other philosophers lacked. As a distraction from work you wrote love songs, both in meter and in rhyme, which, for their sweet sentiment and their melody have been sung and sung again and have kept your name in every mouth. Your lovely melodies prevent even the illiterate from forgetting you. Because of these gifts women sighed for your love. And because these songs celebrated our own love, they quickly spread my name over many lands and made me the envy of womanhood. What mental or physical excellence did not adorn your youth? None of the women who envied me then could now refrain from pitying me, cut off as I am from such delights. Indeed, what enemy of mine would not now be moved by the compassion that I deserve.

I brought you evil, but you must know how innocently I did so. For crime lies in the intention of the doer, not in the result of the act. Justice does not consider what happens but through what intent it happens. My intent toward you only you have known, and only you can judge. I commit everything to your judgment and submit to your decree.

Tell me one thing: why, after our conversion which you commanded, did I sink into oblivion, no more to be refreshed by your speech or your letters? Tell me, I say, if you can, else I will say what I feel and what everybody suspects: desire, not affection, drew you to me; lust, not love. So when desire ceased, whatever you were doing for its sake vanished too. This, my beloved, is not so much my own opinion as the opinion of everyone. If only it were merely mine, and your love might have defenders to argue away my pain. If only I could invent some reason to excuse you and at the same time to cover my cheapness. Listen I beg you to what I ask, and it will seem trifling and easy to you. Since I am cheated of your presence, at least put your promises in words, of which you have such a treasure, and in that way keep before me the sweetness of your image. It will be vain for me to expect you to be bountiful in acts if I find you niggardly in words. Truly I believed that I merited much from you when I had done everything for your sake and continue still in obedience. When little more than a girl I took the hard vows of a nun, not from piety but at your command. If I deserve nothing from you, how vain I regard my labor! Nor can I expect a reward from God, for I have done nothing for love of Him. You, hurrying to God, I followed, or, rather, preceded you. For as you remembered how Lot's wife turned back, you first delivered me to God bound by the vow, and then delivered yourself. That one act of distrust, I confess, sorrowed me and made me blush. God knows, at your command I would have followed or preceded you to the external fires. For my heart is not with me but with you, and now more than ever, if it is not with you it is nowhere, for it cannot exist without you. See to it, I beg you, that my heart may be well with you, and it will be well if it finds you kind, giving grace for grace, a little for much. My beloved, if only your love were less sure of me so that it might be more regarding. I have made you so secure that you are neglectful. Remember all that I have done, and think what you owe me. While I enjoyed bodily joys with you, many people wondered whether I acted from love or lust. Now the end makes the beginning clear. I have cut myself off from pleasure to obey your will. I have kept nothing except to be more than ever yours. Think how wicked you would be, when all the more is owing me, to give me less—almost nothing—especially when so little is asked, and that so easy for you. In the name of God to whom you have vowed yourself, give me of yourself that thing that is possible— the consolation of a letter. Refreshed by it, I swear that I will serve God more readily. Long ago when you used to summon me to pleasures you sought me out with frequent letters and never failed, with your songs, to keep your Héloïse on every tongue. The streets, the houses echoed me. How much more fitting that you should now incite me to God rather than to lust as you did then. Think what you owe; do what I ask. And I will conclude this long letter with a short ending:

Farewell, my only one!

FROM HÉLOÏSE'S SECOND LETTER TO ABELARD

. . . What hope remains for me when you are gone? What reason to continue this pilgrimage, when I have no comfort except you? And of you I have only the bare knowledge that you are alive, for your restoring presence is not granted me. Oh—if it is right to say it—how cruel God has been to me! Inclement clemency! Fortune has exhausted her arrows against me so that others have nothing to fear. Indeed, if a single arrow were left no place could be found in me for another wound. Fortune's only fear is that I escape her torments through death. Wretched and unhappy am I! In you I was raised above all women, and in you am I all the more fatally thrown down. What glory I had in you! What desolation I have now! Fortune made me the happiest of women only that she might make me the most miserable. The injury was all the more outrageous in that all considerations of right and wrong were violated. While we abandoned ourselves to the delights of love the divine severity spared us. When we made our forbidden acts lawful and cleansed the stains of fornication by marriage, the Lord's anger broke upon us, impatient of an innocent bed when it had long tolerated a defiled one. A man caught in adultery would have been amply punished by what happened to you. But what others deserved for adultery, you received from the marriage which you believed made up for everything. Adulteresses bring their lovers what your own wife brought you. You alone paid the penalty for what we had done together, and you paid it not when we lived for pleasure but when we lived in chastity, separated, you presiding at the schools of Paris, I, at your command, living with the nuns at Argenteuil, you devoted to study, I to prayer and devotional reading. Alone you bore the punishment that you deserved less than I. Humiliating yourself and elevating me and all my relatives, you little deserved that punishment either from God or from those traitors. Miserable me, begotten to cause such a crime! Oh womankind, ever the ruin of the noblest men!

The devil well knows how easily a man may fall through a wife. He covered us with his malace, and the man whom he could not cast down through fornication he tried through marriage, using good to bring about evil where evil means had failed. I thank God, at least, that the devil did not lure me to assent to that marriage which became the cause of the wicked deed. Yet although my mind absolves me in this one thing, too many sins had gone before to absolve me of that crime. Long a slave to forbidden joys, I earned the punishment for which I now suffer for past sins. Let us attribute the evil end to bad beginnings. May my penance be appropriate to what I have done, and may my long remorse compensate in some way for the punishment you suffered. What you once suffered in the body, may I, through contrition, bear to the end of life so that I can in that way make amends to you if not to God. Confessing the weaknesses of my most wicked soul, I can find no penitence to offer God, whom I unceasingly accuse of utter cruelty toward you. Rebellious to His rule, I offend Him with my indignation more than I appease Him with my penitence. For it is no sinner's penitence when, however much the body may suffer, the mind retains the will to sin and still burns with the same desires. It is easy to accuse yourself of sin in confession, and easy to do penance with the body. But it is hard indeed to turn your heart away from desiring its greatest joys. The pleasures of love, which we knew together, cannot be made displeasing to me or driven from my memory. Wherever I turn they press upon me, nor do they spare my dreams. Even in the solemn moments of the Mass, when prayer should be purest, their phantoms catch my soul. When I should groan for what I have done, I sigh for what I have lost. Not only our acts, but even the times and places, stick fast in my mind, and my body quivers. Oh most wretched me, fit only to utter this cry of the soul: "Wretched that I am, who will deliver me from the body of this death?" If only I could truthfully add: "I thank God through Jesus Christ our Lord." Such thanksgiving, my dearest, may indeed be yours since by one wound of the body you have been cured of many tortures of the soul, and God may well have been merciful where he seemed to act against you, like a good physician who does not spare the pain needed to save a life. But I am tortured by passion and the fires of memory! . . .

13   FROM   *Etienne Gilson*
           Héloïse and Abélard

The noted intellectual historian Etienne Gilson relates the love of Abelard and Héloïse to the general issue of the "Twelfth-Century Renaissance."

In spite of the many problems still left unsolved in this history of Héloïse and Abélard, there is sufficient information available

SOURCE. Etienne Gilson, *Héloïse and Abélard*, L. K. Shook, tr., Chicago: Henry Regnery Company, 1951, pp. 124–127 and 134. Copyright 1951 by Henry Regnery Company. Reprinted by permission of Henry Regnery Company and the translator.

to make the effort of gathering it all together quite worth while. There are literally hundreds of definitions of the Renaissance, most of which concur in assigning as its essential characteristic, the appearance of strong individuals capable at last of giving expression to their own personality, after centuries of medieval oppression. There is nothing quite comparable to the passion of the historians of the Renaissance for its individualism, its independence of mind, its rebellion against the principle of authority, unless perchance it is the docility with which those same historians copy one another in dogmatizing about the Middle Ages of which they know so little. We should not attach much importance to this attitude, save that those who speak thus of things they understand so poorly pretend to act in defense of reason and of personal observation. Their charge that all those who hold a different opinion are yielding to prejudice would, indeed, be sad, were it not so comic. Indifference to facts, distrust of direct observation and personal knowledge, the tendency to prune their data to suit their hypotheses, the naïve and dogmatic tendency to charge that those who would refute their position with self-evident facts lack a critical sense—these are the substance of their charge against the Middle Ages. Certainly, the Middle Ages had its fair share of these limitations. But at the same time these same limitations provide a perfect picture of the attitude of these historians of the Renaissance. They themselves possess the weaknesses of which they accuse the Middle Ages.

For Jacob Burckhardt, who only echoes the Preface to Volume VII of Michelet's *History of France*, the Renaissance is characterized by the discovery of the world and by the discovery of man. "To the discovery of the outward world the Renaissance added a still greater achievement by first discerning and bringing to light the full, whole nature of man." Once the principle is stated, the consequences follow of themselves: "This period, as we have seen, first gave the highest development to individuality, and then led the individual to the most zealous and thorough study of himself in all forms and under all conditions." It is therefore the great poets of the fourteenth century whom he first discusses as providing a "free delineation of the human spirit," or as the French translator puts it, "of the moral man," and above all Dante who established a "boundary between medievalism and modern times."

It is perhaps true, as Ernest Renan and Pierre de Nolhac say, that Petrarch was the first of the moderns. But what does it matter? Are we for all this any nearer the first modern man? For Burckhardt this is not the essential thing. What he wishes to prove before everything else is that such strong individuals could only have appeared first in the tiny Italian tyrannies of the fourteenth century where men led so intense a personal life that they had to talk about it. And so we read that "Even autobiography (and not merely history) takes here and there in Italy a bold and vigorous flight, and puts before us, together with the most varied incidents of external life, striking revelations of the inner man. Among other nations, even in Germany, at the time of the Reformation, it deals only with outward experiences, and leaves us to guess at the spirit within. It seems as though Dante's *La Vita nuova*, with the inexorable truthfulness that runs through it, had shown his people the way." We can, moreover, find a reason for this absence of individuality among medieval folk. Need we speak it? It is to be found in the subjugation and standardization which Christianity forced upon them. "Once mistress, the Church does not tolerate the development of the individual. All must be resigned to becoming simple links in her long chain and to obeying the laws of her institutions."

A man lacking individuality, incapable of analyzing himself, without the taste for describing others in biography or himself in autobiography, such is the man Christianity produces. Let us cite, as an example, St. Augustine! But to confine ourselves to the twelfth century, and without asking from what unique mould we could fashion at the same time a Bernard of Clairvaux and a Pierre Abélard, let us make a simple comparison between the Renaissance of the professors and the facts which become manifest in the correspondence of Héloïse and Abélard.

If all we need for a Renaissance is to find individuals developed to the highest point, does not this pair suffice? To be sure, Abélard and Héloïse are not Italians. They were not born in some tiny Tuscan "tyranny" of the fourteenth century. They satisfy, in brief, none of the conditions which the theory demands except that they were just what they ought not to have been if the theory were true. One insists, however, upon persons capable of "freely describing the moral man," even as the great Italians could do it.

Perhaps even here Abélard and Héloïse labored with some suc-
cess! No one would be so foolish as to compare their correspondence with the *Vita nuova* as literature. But if it is just a matter
of stating in which of the two works one finds the moral man
more simply and more directly described, the tables are turned.
It is the *Vita nuova* that can no longer bear the comparison.
Historians still wonder whether Beatrice was a little Florentine
or a symbol. But there is nothing symbolic about Héloïse, nor
was her love for Abélard but the unfolding of allegorical remarks.
This story of flesh and blood, carried along by a passion at once
brutal and ardent to its celebrated conclusion, we know from
within as, indeed, we know few others. Its heroes observe themselves, analyze themselves as only Christian consciences fallen
prey to passions can do it. Nor do they merely analyze themselves,
but they talk about themselves as well. What Renaissance auto-
biographies can be compared with the correspondence of Abélard
and Héloïse? Perchance Benvenuto Cellini's? But even Burckhardt
recognizes that this does not claim to be "founded on introspec-
tion." Moreover, the reader "often detects him bragging or lying."
On the contrary, it is absolutely certain that it is their inmost
selves about which Abélard and Héloïse instruct us; and if they
sometimes lie to themselves, they never lie to us. . . .

   No text seems better able to give a due sense of the complexity
of these problems to those anxious to acquire it than the correspondence of Héloïse and Abélard. As Nordström rightly says:
"If we had only these precious documents to reveal the penetrat-
ing and realistic power of auto-analysis in a medieval man, they
would be adequate to demonstrate the fundamental error of
Burckhardt when he tells us that Dante was the first to reveal
frankly the mysteries of his interior life and thus inaugurate a
new epoch in the history of the development of the European
man." It could not be put better. Only let us add that if Abélard
is a fatal obstacle to Burckhardt's thesis, Héloïse is in her own
right a far more dangerous one, not so much because of the passionate ardor with which she analyzes herself, nor of the defiant
air with which she publishes her most intimate secrets, but because of the ideas she expresses and the very content of what
she says.

ARCHITECTURE AND SCULPTURE

14   *Romanesque Exterior*
    Façade of Notre Dame la Grande, Poitiers

One of the most original achievements of the "Twelfth-Century
Renaissance" occurred in the related fields of architecture and sculpture. The period witnessed the development and perfection of two
great artistic styles: the Romanesque and the Gothic. When the
period opened, the Gothic style was unknown; at its close, most of
the great high Gothic cathedrals were completed or underway.

The Romanesque and Gothic achievements are difficult to relate
to the renaissance problem. If splendid originality and the creation of
beauty are sufficient credentials, then in the area of architecture and
sculpture the "Twelfth-Century Renaissance" was a renaissance indeed. But if classicism is to be the touchstone, then the Romanesque
style must be regarded as a far less perfect imitation of Roman
architecture than the more studiously classical buildings of the later
Renaissance. And the Gothic style, radically unclassical and all the
more original for that, would disqualify the period 1150-1250 from
any claim to "renaissance" status. Yet if Chartres is to be "disqualified"
because it does not resemble the Roman Pantheon, one might well
conclude that the non-renaissances are at least as interesting and fruitful
as the renaissances.

Our section on architecture and sculpture begins with three illustrations of the fully developed Romanesque style of the late-eleventh
and early-twelfth centuries. The west façade of Notre Dame la
Grande, Poitiers, illustrates the consistent use of the Roman round
arch, the earthbound solidity of the total architectural mass, and the
rich, relatively distorted, rigorously architectonic quality of the sculp-

*ture. The work of the sculptor is strictly subordinated to the archi-
tecture of the building. The Romanesque style embodied a fusion
of architecture and sculpture—a unity based upon the medium of
stone.*

SOURCE. Marburg–Art Reference Bureau.

15   *Romanesque Interior*
           Notre Dame la Porte, Clermont-Ferrand

*By the standards of the later Gothic style, the Romanesque interior
is dark—characterized by heavy masses and relatively small windows.
The interior sculpture is by and large limited to the capitals of
columns, where it often displays a fantastic inventiveness. The round
arch is omnipresent, and the roof is usually vaulted in stone, supported
by thick walls and sturdy columns or piers. The style is graceful and
richly decorated in southern Europe but tends to become increasingly
severe and stolid as one moves northward. Notre Dame la Porte, in
central France, falls between these two extremes. (The pier statues
were added at a much later date.)*

SOURCE. Marburg—Art Reference Bureau.

16   *Romanesque Sculpture*
Tympanum, Conques, and Narthex Capital, St.
Benoît-sur-Loire

These examples of early twelfth-century Romanesque sculpture demonstrate further the subordination of realism to symbolic message and architectural space. The Conques tympanum, dating from about 1130, is characteristic in several respects: tympanum sculpture is common in Romanesque churches, and the Last Judgment is a recurring theme. Note the unclassical element of fantasy and exaggeration in the depiction of human, humanoid, and animal forms.

SOURCE. Both, Marburg–Art Reference Bureau.

17   *Late Romanesque Interior*
            Nave, Durham Cathedral

The plan of this structure dates from the end of the eleventh century and the early years of the twelfth. It is unquestionably a Romanesque church—and a superb example of the stark power of the Norman Romanesque style, imported to England after the Conquest of 1066. Durham is of unique architectural interest in that it is the first known structure in Western Europe to employ the ribbed vault and the pointed arch (in the great transverse arches of the vault). These two elements became dominant in the Gothic style.

SOURCE. Marburg—Art Reference Bureau.

18   *Transitional Interior*
              Nave, Le Mans Cathedral

Several decades have passed since the building of the choir and nave of Durham. The earthbound heaviness of the Romanesque style is still present in the Le Mans nave of the mid-twelfth century, but the arcade arches are now bluntly pointed. This nave also contains some of Europe's earliest stained glass. The "Twelfth-Century Renaissance" witnessed the first extensive use of this luminous medium, and the beauty of stained glass such as is found at Le Mans may well have stimulated the Gothic cathedral builders in their endeavor to create ever-larger windows.

SOURCE. Marburg—Art Reference Bureau.

19   *Early Gothic Interior*
                      Nave, Laon Cathedral

*In this early Gothic cathedral of northern France, dating from the
third quarter of the twelfth century, the pointed arch and ribbed
vault have become prominent. The shift has occurred from the
Romanesque program of heavy stone vaulting supported by thick
walls and columns to the Gothic program in which weights and
stresses are carried by ribs, slender columns, and graceful buttresses.
The Gothic structure is, in essence, a skeleton in which walls become
screens—structurally unnecessary—and, as time goes on, are opened
increasingly into windows of stained glass.*

*Laon Cathedral, being early in the Gothic period, does not exploit
Gothic structural possibilities to the fullest. It is a fascinating church
in its bold originality, yet it seems somewhat unsure, heavy, with a
touch of the Romanesque feeling remaining. The four-story elevation
was a transitional experiment, not altogether successful, and later
Gothic churches returned to the Romanesque three-story system of
arcades, triforium, and clerestory. As the Gothic age proceeded, the
clerestory windows, filled with colored glass, became increasingly
large.*

SOURCE. Marburg—Art Reference Bureau.

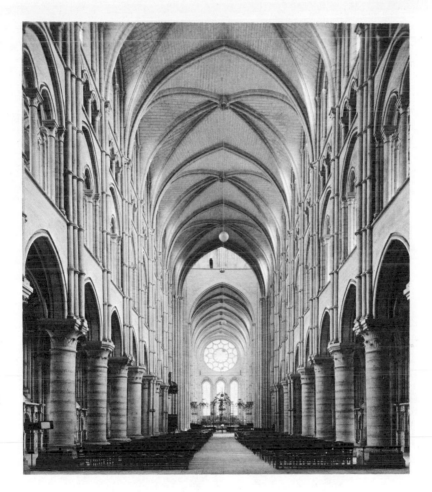

20   *Late Transitional Sculpture*
           Royal Portal, Chartres

This superb example of later twelfth-century sculpture is much closer to the coming Gothic style than to the earlier Romanesque. The human figures are far taller, nobler, and more lifelike. Sculpture is breaking free of architectural surfaces and coming into its own. Romanesque fantasy is giving way to a serene, idealized naturalism.

SOURCE. Marburg—Art Reference Bureau.

21   *High Gothic Sculpture*
            South Porch, Chartres

This sculpture, dating from the early thirteenth century, epitomizes the Gothic style at its noblest and most assured. The reader might ask himself, in examining this style, whether or not "humanistic" would be an appropriate adjective to describe it, and why. There is no approved answer, but the question might well lead to a clearer understanding of the various possible meanings of the term "humanism."

SOURCE. Marburg–Art Reference Bureau.

22   *High Gothic Exterior*
Facade and Chevet, Notre Dame, Paris

The portions of Notre Dame, Paris, illustrated here typify the Gothic architecture of the early thirteenth century. The chevet (rounded east end of the church) is characteristically Gothic in its use of flying buttresses as a part of the skeletal structural framework. The Gothic architects did not hide their structural scheme but displayed it for all to see. Indeed, the flying buttresses here are much larger and more conspicuous than structural necessity demanded.

SOURCE. Both, Marburg—Art Reference Bureau.

23   *High Gothic Interior*
Choir and Nave, Reims Cathedral

Built for the most part in the early thirteenth century, Reims cathedral is a splendid example of the high Gothic style, with high, pointed aisle arches, lofty ribbed vaulting, and huge clerestory windows. The total effect is utterly different from that of Greco-Roman architecture, even though the capitals of the Reims arcade columns are classical in feeling. The sense of drama and upward-reaching, expressive of the religious aspirations of the early thirteenth century, was considered vulgar and barbaric by artists of the Italian Renaissance.

SOURCE. Marburg—Art Reference Bureau.

24   *Italian Renaissance Exterior*
          Façade, St. Andrea, Mantua

   *Built in the late fifteenth century on a plan by Leon Battista
Alberti, this church illustrates the Italian Renaissance's return to
classical models. Much more classical in style and mood than any
Romanesque church and infinitely more so than the high Gothic
cathedrals, St. Andrea is considered one of the architectural master-
pieces of Renaissance Italy. It bears witness to a radically different
system of artistic values than that of the "Twelfth-Century Renaissance."*

SOURCE. Marburg—Art Reference Bureau.

RATIONALISM

25 FROM   R. W. Southern
The Making of the Middle Ages

The rise of rationalism in high medieval thought is, again, an ambiguous phenomenon in terms of the renaissance problem. The twelfth century was an age of high hopes for the triumph of reason over the unknown, and in its later decades scholars turned increasingly to the field of logic—or dialectic as it was then called. Science, too, was beginning to attract first-rate minds, and scientific knowledge was being collected and studied as a prelude to the important creative advances in scientific methodology of such thirteenth-century scholars as Robert Grosseteste and Roger Bacon. Renaissance Italy, on the other hand, was not notably productive in the areas of scientific theory and technical philosophy.

Yet the science and dialectic of the later twelfth and thirteenth centuries was accompanied by a decline in the study of classical letters—or, as most historians would describe it, a decline in "humanism." Renaissance "humanism," in other words, gave way in the later twelfth century to non-renaissance logic, though that logic was rooted in Greek philosophy.

In the following passage the distinguished English medievalist R. W. Southern discusses the impact of translations from the Arabic and Greek on the intellectual revival of the High Middle Ages.

SOURCE. R. W. Southern, *The Making of the Middle Ages*, New Haven: Yale University Press, 1953, pp. 63–68. Copyright 1953 by Yale University Press. Reprinted by permission of Yale University Press.

When men in western Europe between 1098 and 1204 wrote of the wealth of Constantinople they were generally referring not so much to its stores of gold and precious stuffs as to a less material form of wealth: its spiritual wealth. And when they talked of its spiritual wealth, they were generally thinking not of its stores of ancient literature, or of the acquaintance with the works of antiquity which was to be found among cultivated people in the Eastern capital, but of the prodigious stores of relics which were reported to be possessed by the churches of the city. The unworthiness of the Byzantines to be the custodians of this sacred treasure was one of the arguments by which the Crusaders' assault on the city was justified. Naturally, therefore, the fall of the city led to a wide dispersal of this wealth throughout the churches of the West. Many of the objects which were held in particular veneration in the thirteenth century—the Holy Rood at Bromholm, the Holy Blood at Westminster, the Crown of Thorns at Paris—came to these places directly or indirectly as a result of the events of 1204. It was through these objects of devotion that the fall of Constantinople entered into the lives of many people who had no further concern with the Empire or its fate.

There is no legend of the widespread transfer of Greek books and literature to the West as a result of the fall of Constantinople in 1204. It might be inferred from this that there was a lack of interest in the thought and literature of ancient Greece, of which Constantinople was the chief guardian, and to the influence of which Byzantine civilization was the living witness. But this is not so. There was certainly little or no interest in Greek letters, such as there was two and a half centuries later: but among a small circle of scholars there was, and had been for more than a century, intense interest in the results of Greek scientific and philosophical enquiry. For every one person interested in Greek thought there were perhaps a hundred interested in Byzantine relics, but this small class of scholars was busy re-laying the foundations of western science. Nor were they blind to the part which Constantinople could play in providing material for this work, as a single illustration will show.

One of the most important events in the history of the twelfth-century scientific thought was the translation into Latin of

Ptolemy's *Almagest*. This was a work which superseded all the books of astronomy at that time known to the West. It is therefore interesting to find that it was first known to the Latin world by means of a copy brought from Constantinople to Palermo about 1160, as a present from the Eastern Emperor to the King of Sicily, in the course of some diplomatic exchanges. Even more interesting is the discovery made by the late Professor Haskins that it was first translated into Latin by a scholar, who heard of the arrival of the manuscript while he was studying medicine at Salerno, and straightway hurried across to Sicily to catch a sight of the great work. The intellectual wealth of Constantinople was therefore not unknown, and the news of the arrival of an important scientific work travelled far and could arouse great enthusiasm.

Why then was Constantinople not more valued as an intellectual treasure house? The answer is twofold. In the first place, though the Latins were interested in Greek science, and some at least of them were prepared to go to great lengths to obtain the scientific works of antiquity, they were not at all interested in the literary culture of Byzantium; and even if they had been, they had not enough Greek to make it accessible to them. At Constantinople science had stood still, but nearer home there were centres of learning where the ancient Greek scientific works were available, and where a body of scientific teaching had grown out of them which was greatly desired for its own sake. These were the centres which had developed under Moslem rule in Spain and Sicily. The drawback that the Greek works were here found at one remove from their original language— in Arabic—was more than balanced by finding them surrounded by a body of living thought. There was also what appears to us a strange blindness among the Latins to the disadvantages of making translations from translations: their standards of translation were not high, and they probably depended more than we know on discussion and verbal explanation, rather than on the mere letter of the text. Hence the Arabic contribution to western thought was, during our period, far more valued and far more impressive than the Byzantine contribution. The fate of the translation of the *Almagest* which has just been mentioned is significant in this respect: although the first translation was made directly from the Greek, this translation soon disappeared from sight, and its place in general esteem throughout the Middle Ages was taken by a translation from the Arabic made some fifteen years later.

This fruitful contact between the Moslem and Christian worlds developed after the beginning of our period, and its greatest days were over by the time our period ends.[1] At the very end of the tenth century the first faint traces of Moslem influence on Christendom are to be found in some Arabic numerals in two Latin manuscripts, which had their origin on the Spanish border. These numerals are a curiosity at this time for they did not become common in western Europe until the fourteenth century; but they show that the silent penetration had begun. We can be sure that it had not begun much earlier because between about 960 and 970 the greatest scholar in Europe lived in Northern Spain without feeling in any noticeable way the impact of Arabic studies. Gerbert (the later Pope Silvester II) was possessed by an avidity for books and learning which made him scour the libraries of Europe for unknown texts, with an enthusiasm reminiscent of the later searches of Renaissance scholars. He had gone to the border country near Barcelona for the express purpose of studying; and two of his favourite subjects—mathematics and astronomy—had been intensively cultivated by Moslem scholars. But he left without knowing anything of their discoveries in these fields. The body of knowledge on which he built his reputation in later years was entirely of Latin origin.

Between Silvester II[2] and Innocent III[3] every generation saw some fresh addition to the scientific knowledge which Latin scholars owed to Arabic sources. Gerbert's own pupils were in possession of one of the major contributions to science which came by this channel: they possessed the instrument known as the astrolabe which for the first time made possible accurate measurements of the elevation of the stars. During the next generation, in the middle years of the eleventh century, the stream of

[1] The period referred to here runs from 972 to the capture of Constantinople in 1204.

[2] Pope, 999–1003.

[3] Pope, 1198–1216.

medical learning, of which the principal centre at this time was the South Italian health resort at Salerno, began to flow from Arabic into Latin.

These were only the beginnings of a one-way traffic in ideas which, hesitatingly in the eleventh century, but with rapidly increasing impetus throughout the twelfth century, transformed the scientific knowledge of the Latin West. Wherever the receding tide of Moslem or Byzantine power, in Spain, Sicily and Southern Italy, left men who knew Arabic or Greek and could serve as intermediaries between Christendom and the outside world, there were Latin scholars anxious to make use of their new opportunities. Scholars came to these centres from England, France and Italy in search of knowledge; and slowly by their efforts and those of their collaborators a new scientific library was built up more extensive than that which the Latin world had ever known.

It may help to give some idea of the extent of the revolution which was thus effected to make a brief comparison between the scientific works which were available in Latin to scholars in various subjects at the beginning and end of our period.

Taking the "literary" subjects (grammar, rhetoric and logic) first, there is no great change to record except in logic: here the scholar owed all the more advanced books of Aristotle (the *Prior and Posterior Analytics*, the *Topics* and *Sophistici Elenchi*) to translations made during our period from Greek or Arabic or from both. Yet the revolution here was not as great as this broad change might make it appear; for though these books of Aristotle had previously been unknown, the outline of his doctrine was . . . accessible to the tenth-century scholar from other sources. It is when we come to the scientific subjects that the change in the position is so great as to sweep away the old landmarks: in mathematics the study of geometry had been practically founded by the translation of Euclid in the early twelfth century; in astronomy the fragmentary reports contained in Latin writers on the seven arts such as Martianus Capella had been replaced by the fundamental work of Ptolemy, the translation of which has already been mentioned. In medicine, the translations of the works of Galen and Hippocrates and a whole host of Arabic writers—largely the result of the indefatigable labours of one man, Gerard of Cremona, working in Toledo between 1175 and 1187—had entirely superseded the few elementary works available at the beginning of this period: a well-stocked medical library of the thirteenth century might well have contained no single work known to the Latin world two centuries earlier. Beyond these subjects there was a range of sciences which had no place in tenth-century schemes of knowledge: physics, optics, mechanics, biology—all of them had their origin, so far as Latin Europe was concerned, in translations from Greek and Arabic made during the twelfth century. In 972 none of Aristotle's works on natural science were known in Latin. By 1204, there were translations (in several cases, more than one translation) of Aristotle's works on Physics, on the Heavens, on Meteorology, on the Soul, on Sensation, on Memory and Remembering, on Sleeping and Waking, on Longevity and its opposite, on Youth and Old Age, on Respiration, on Life and Death. So far as we know, all these translations were made in the half century between about 1150 and 1200; and to this body of scientific works which made their way into Christendom in this brief time, we should add the works of Moslem scholars, who henceforth became familiar in the West under strange names—Albumazar, Alfragani, Alfarabi, Avicenna, and soon, and most potent of all, Averroës.

It is clear that these changes constitute a considerable revolution, made possible by the changing relations between Latin Europe and its neighbours during our period. Despite the Crusades—partly even as a result of the Crusades—Christian and Moslem scholars met on common ground in scientific enquiry. The large-scale hostility produced or permitted a measure of collaboration which had been quite unknown in the tenth century. The case was similar with regard to the Jews, who played a notable part in the work of translation and interpretation: here also the twelfth century witnessed an appalling development in outbreaks of hysterical violence against the Jewish community—and, at the same time, many acts of individual co-operation for scientific ends. The heightening of tension between Christendom and the bodies which existed outside it was one symptom of

Rationalism 143

that growth in power and confidence, of which the pursuit of scientific knowledge beyond the ancient boundaries of the Latin tradition was another.

One is tempted to add that the collaboration was of more permanent importance than the hostility. Perhaps it was, but the importance of the activities which have just been described lay in the future. Most of the developments in thought and experience which we shall have to describe later in this book drew their strength from the native tradition of Latin Europe, and owed little to the science which became available in the translations of our period. The work of translation and even of comprehension is after all only a first step; it remained to be seen to what use these translations would be put, and how they would affect the general conditions of thought among scholars and among that wider public which studied but left no name in the history of scholarship. This story belongs to the thirteenth and later centuries. Before the end of our period we can record no single scientific name, no pregnant idea or observation in the field of science, which emerged from the great labours of research and translation. This is only what might be expected: the new world had to be discovered before it could be settled. These translations represented a great adventure in exploration opening out a world quite as new as that which was discovered by the voyagers of the fifteenth and sixteenth centuries. A great wealth of new knowledge was unearthed, but (for all the explorers knew) treasures far richer than any which were ever to be discovered might have lurked in the next book to be turned from Greek or Arabic into Latin. By 1204 the great period of acquisition was coming to an end: the period of digestion was beginning.

26   *Adelard of Bath*
                Natural Questions

Adelard of Bath, an English scholar of the early twelfth century,
spent some time studying abroad and was an important transmitter
of Arabic (and, indirectly, Greek) scientific ideas into the West. In
the following excerpts, Adelard expresses an intense commitment to
reason—an attitude that was to become steadily more widespread as
the century progressed.

On my return the other day to England, in the reign of Henry,
son of William[1]—it was he who had long maintained me abroad
for the purpose of study—the renewal of intercourse with my
friends gave me both pleasure and benefit.

After the first natural enquiries about my own health and that
of my friends, my particular desire was to learn all I could about
the manners and customs of my own country. Making this then
the object of my enquiry, I learnt that its chief men were violent,
its magistrates wine-lovers, its judges mercenary; that patrons
were fickle, private men sycophants, those who made promises
deceitful, friends full of jealousy, and almost all men self-seekers:[2]
this realised, the only resource, I said to myself, is to withdraw
my thoughts from all misery.

Thereupon my friends said to me, "What do you think of
doing, since you neither wish to adopt this moral depravity
yourself, nor can you prevent it?" My reply was "to give myself
up to oblivion, since oblivion is the only cure for evils that cannot be remedied; for he who gives heed to that which he hates
in some sort endures that which he does not love." Thus we

---

[1] King Henry I, 1100–1135, son of William the Conqueror.
[2] This passage is a significant demonstration of the essential continuity of
human nature.
SOURCE. Adelard of Bath, *Dodi Ve-Nechdi, The Work of Berachya*
Hanakdan, Sir Hermann Gollancz, tr., London: Oxford University Press,
1920, pp. 91–92 and 98–99. Copyright 1920 by Oxford University Press.

argued that matter together, and then as we still had time left
for talking, a certain nephew of mine, who had come along with
the others, rather adding to the tangle than unravelling it, urged
me to publish something fresh in the way of Arabian learning.
As the rest agreed with him, I took in hand the treatise which
follows: of its profitableness to its readers I am assured, but am
doubtful whether it will give them pleasure. The present generation has this ingrained weakness, that it thinks that nothing discovered by the moderns is worthy to be received—the result of
this is that if I wanted to publish anything of my own invention
I should attribute it to someone else, and say, "Someone else said
this, not I." Therefore (that I may not wholly be robbed of a
hearing) it was a certain great man that discovered all my
ideas, not I. But of this enough.

Since I have yielded to the request of my friends so far as to
write something, it remains for you to give your judgment as to
its correctness. About this point I would that I felt less anxiety,
for there is no essay in the liberal arts, no matter how well handled, to which you could not give a wider range. Grant me,
therefore, your sympathy. I shall now proceed to give short
answers to questions put by my nephew. . . .

NEPHEW: To me it seems that you go too far in your praise of
the Arabs, and show prejudice in your disparagement of the
learning of our philosophers. Our reward will be that you will
have gained some fruit of your toil; if you give good answers, and
I make a good showing as your opponent, you will see that my
promise has been well kept.

ADELARD: You perhaps take a little more on you than you ought,
but as this arrangement will be profitable not only to you but to
many others, I will pardon your forwardness, making however
this one stipulation, that when I adduce something unfamiliar,
people are to think not that I am putting forward an idea of my
own, but am giving the views of the Arabs. If anything I say
displeases the less educated, I do not want them to be displeased
with me also: I know too well what is the fate which attends
upon the teachers of the truth with the common herd, and consequently shall plead the case of the Arabs, not my own.

NEPHEW: Let it be as you will, provided nothing causes you to
hold your peace. . . .

ADELARD: It is a little difficult for you and me to argue about animals. I, with reason for my guide, have learned one thing from my Arab teachers, you, something different; dazzled by the outward show of authority you wear a head-stall. For what else should we call authority but a head-stall? Just as brute animals are led by the head-stall where one pleases, without seeing why or where they are being led, and only follow the halter by which they are held, so many of you, bound and fettered as you are by a low credulity, are led into danger by the authority of writers. Hence, certain people arrogating to themselves the title of authorities have employed an unbounded licence in writing, and this to such an extent that they have not hesitated to insinuate into men of low intellect the false instead of the true. Why should you not fill sheets of paper, aye, fill them on both sides, when to-day you can get readers who require no proof of sound judgment from you, and are satisfied merely with the name of a time-worn title? They do not understand that reason has been given to individuals that, with it as chief judge, distinction may be drawn between the true and the false. Unless reason were appointed to be the chief judge, to no purpose would she have been given to us individually: it would have been enough for the writing of laws to have been entrusted to one, or at most to a few, and the rest would have been satisfied with their ordinances and authority. Further, the very people who are called authorities first gained the confidence of their inferiors only because they followed reason; and those who are ignorant of reason, or neglect it, justly desire to be called blind. However, I will not pursue this subject any further, though I regard authority as matter for contempt. This one thing, however, I will say. We must first search after reason, and when it has been found, and not until then, authority if added to it, may be received. Authority by itself can inspire no confidence in the philosopher, nor ought it to be used for such a purpose. Hence logicians have agreed in treating the argument from authority not as necessary, but probable only. If, therefore, you want to hear anything from me, you must both give and take reason.

27 FROM   *Dom David Knowles*
      The Evolution of Medieval Thought

The English church historian Dom David Knowles discusses here in broad perspective the intellectual awakening of high medieval Europe.

Although the myth of a Christendom awaiting imminent dissolution in the year 999, and surging forward in relief in 1001, has been effectively banished from serious historical writing, the millenary year, coinciding as it did with part of the brief pontificate of Silvester II, the most learned man of his day in Europe, is an easy and convenient date to mark the opening of a new epoch. The great revival of the eleventh century, which gathered amplitude and momentum in the twelfth century, and reached its highest and most characteristic, though not perhaps its most universal, achievement in the thirteenth century, was manifest in all contemporary mental activities and affected theology, philosophy, religious reform, both public and private, literature as well in poetry as in prose, architecture, sculpture, illumination, law both canon and civil, mathematics and the natural sciences. Here we are not concerned with art, and can consider mathematics and science only incidentally; our principal concern is with thought, and more superficially with literature and law in so far as they reflect thought.

In all the departments of mental activity that have been mentioned there was a simultaneous renaissance and a parallel, though not in every case an equally swift or extensive, advance. Thus the period 1000-1150 was distinguished primarily by a literary renaissance, culminating in the age of the great historians, hu-

SOURCE. Dom David Knowles, *The Evolution of Medieval Thought*, Baltimore: Helicon Press, 1962, pp. 79–83. Copyright 1962 by Dom David Knowles. Excerpted with permission of Helicon Press, Inc., Baltimore, Maryland and Longmans, Green and Company Limited.

manists, preachers and letter-writers of the age of St. Bernard, William of Malmesbury and John of Salisbury. Thenceforward, Latin letters declined. Philosophy and theology, on the other hand, developed slowly but steadily from 1050 onwards, reaching their fullest expansion only between 1220 and 1350, after which a rapid decline began. Law, for its part, grew steadily in importance during the eleventh century, made its most spectacular advances in the middle decades of the twelfth century, and continued as an influential discipline, though without striking developments and changes, until the end of the Middle Ages and beyond.

This great European revival had certain leading characteristics which help the historian to describe its course.

It was in origin confined to the regions covered by the modern countries of France and Belgium and the northern Italian district of Lombardy; it subsequently spread to and absorbed Great Britain south of the Firth of Forth, southern and western Germany, central and south Italy and Sicily, and part of northern Spain. It is, however, remarkable that there was no national or political focus, and for more than a century it was officially fostered by neither pope nor emperor, and patronized neither by a monarch nor by an aristocracy. It was in every sense of the word a supra-national movement, forming a republic of teachers, thinkers and writers. It had the characteristic, peculiar to itself in the history of Western Europe, of becoming in its final development a supra-racial, yet wholly homogeneous, culture. For three hundred years, from 1050 to 1350, and above all in the century between 1070 and 1170, the whole of educated Western Europe formed a single undifferentiated cultural unit. In the lands between Edinburgh and Palermo, Mainz or Lund and Toledo, a man of any city or village might go for education to any school, and become a prelate or an official in any church, court or university (when these existed) from north to south, from east to west. It is the age of Lanfranc of Pavia, Bec and Canterbury, of Anselm of Aosta, Bec and Canterbury, of Vacarius of Lombardy, Canterbury, Oxford and York, of Hugh of Avalon, Witham and Lincoln, of John of Salisbury, Paris, Benevento, Canterbury and Chartres, of Nicholas Brakespeare of St. Albans, France, Scandinavia and Rome, of Thomas of Aquino,

Cologne, Paris and Naples, of Duns Scotus of Dumfries, Oxford,
Paris, and Cologne, of William of Ockham, Oxford, Avignon
and Munich. In this period a high proportion of the most celebrated writers, thinkers and administrators gained greatest fame
and accomplished the most significant part of their life's work
far from the land of their birth and boyhood. Moreover, in the
writings of all those who have just been named, there is not a
single characteristic of language, style or thought to tell us
whence they sprang. True, we are speaking only of a small educated minority, to which the land-owning aristocracy in general,
many monarchs, and even some bishops, did not belong. The
world of Church and State was often rent by schisms and wars,
while the bulk of the population, fast rooted in the soil, knew
nothing beyond the fields and woods of their small corner. But
on the level of literature and thought there was one stock of
words, forms and thoughts from which all drew and in which
all shared on an equality. If we possessed the written works without their authors' names we should not be able to assign them
to any country or people. If we contrast the group of writers
mentioned above with half-a-dozen eminent contemporaries of
the unusually stable European culture of the eighteenth century—
with such men as Kant, Hume, Johnson, Voltaire, Goethe, John
Wesley and St. Alfonso de' Liguori—we shall immediately feel
the difference. Each of the former group is intellectually "state-
less"; each of the latter group has something regional about him.

Yet within the ring-fence of this common culture, movements,
institutions and pursuits varied and developed from place to
place and from time to time. Thus, speaking very generally, and
excluding the largely homeless and rootless group of the Roman
curia, the highest mental activity south of the Alps was urban
and largely lay, and found its most typical expression in medicine
and law. This, the north Italian culture, had an important spill-
over into Provence. North and west of the Alps, on the other
hand, the revival in the first century was wholly clerical and
monastic; it had its centres in the monasteries and cathedral
cities, and found its highest and most typical expression in philosophy and theology.

Speaking still more generally, and regarding the dynamics of
the revival, we can see a steady shift northward to the centre

of gravity. In the middle decades of the eleventh century Salerno, Monte Cassino and the Roman curia were in the van of the advance. Fifty years later the leadership had shifted to Bologna, and before the end of the century France was becoming the schoolmistress of Europe. At the end of the next century Paris was firmly established as the intellectual centre of Europe, and if she remained in pride of place for a century more, other schools, such as Cologne and Oxford, drew level, and for a few decades in the middle of the fourteenth century the two English universities between them perhaps surpassed Paris in their galaxy of talent. Yet if the centre of gravity shifted, men of the most diverse provenance would be constantly found at every point of importance. At the beginning of the fourteenth century both Duns the Scotsman and Marsilio the Paduan left their mark on Paris.

There is a comparable shift in balance if we consider the institutions, the practitioners and the disciplines of this culture. As regards institutions, the organs or instruments of education were: the monastery from 1000 to c. 1150; the cathedral school from 1000 to 1200; the individual master from 1050 to 1150; and the university from 1150 onwards in Italy, and from 1200 onwards in France. These various types of education were reflected in the classes who frequented them. The eleventh century was still primarily the age of the monks, though the secular clerks were growing in numbers at the cathedral schools; the twelfth century was the age of the secular masters and clerks and of the lawyers; in the thirteenth and early fourteenth centuries these classes were still very numerous, but in many of the most celebrated universities the class that gave distinction and set the tone in all matters of philosophy and theology was a new one, that of the friars. As regards the disciplines in fashion, the mental atmosphere of the eleventh century was predominantly literary and humanistic; humanism reached its finest point early in the following century, but already dialectic and speculative theology had become more and more attractive and absorbing and universal in their appeal. From about 1175 they had completely ousted the old literary culture; in the thirteenth century philosophy in all its branches began for the first time to find for itself a curriculum and a discipline that made it an alternative to, and not merely a preparation for theology, and henceforward the two drifted more and more apart.

No adequate cause can be assigned for this great reawakening. Those which have been proposed, such as the return of peace to Western Europe, with a consequent growth of ordered government, wealth and leisure, are certainly not the originating causes of such a widespread, permanent and dynamic change; they are scarcely even necessary conditions. The revival can best be described by a simile: it was the psychological and intellectual adolescence of the new races in Europe. Just as the awakening of the powers of criticism, and a new potentiality of emotion, come in the life of the normal individual, though not always at precisely the same age, so here something analogous occurred in a group of peoples. If we leave the realm of simile, we may say that about A.D. 1000 in north-western Europe, just as in the peoples around the Aegean sea c. 1000 B.C., the elements that combine to produce the mental and psychological qualities of man began to group and blend in a peculiarly harmonious way. The parallel with ancient Greece is indeed very striking. There, as in medieval Europe, the intellectual rebirth cannot be tied down to a single moment or assigned to a single cradle, it appears everywhere within a very wide area; in Greece, as in Europe, a principal part was ultimately taken by dialectic and speculative thought, and there sprang up everywhere men of the most acute mental perception; in Greece also, before and during the lifetime of Socrates and Plato, the weapons of logic and dialectic were turned against venerable institutions and doctrines, as they were in medieval France; there, as here, a great body of logic, metaphysics and ethics was built up; there, as here, a sceptical and opportunist school of thought succeeded in breaking the fabric of thought constructed by the great creative masters, in Greece, Plato and Aristotle, in Europe, St. Bonaventure and St. Thomas.

28 FROM   *G. G. Coulton*
                   Medieval Panorama

*G. G. Coulton, a prolific scholar of medieval social and intellectual
history, points out some of the shortcomings of high medieval thought.
His analysis runs past the close of the period under consideration
here (c. 1050-c. 1250), and deals with such later figures as the mid-
thirteenth-century philosoper St. Thomas Aquinas and the early-
fourteenth-century philosopher William of Ockham. His criticism
of "bibliolatry," however, applies with equal force to the philosophical speculation of the "Twelfth-Century Renaissance."*

The studies of the medieval university were nearly always
based upon the "Arts" course. Medieval philosophy followed
Aristotle in its division of Arts into the "mechanical" and the
"liberal." Mechanical were all that needed manual dexterity, from
the cobbler and saddler to the painter and sculptor: indeed, many
modern artists, from William Morris to Eric Gill, insist upon
this as the only sane definition. Liberal were the arts concerned
only with brain-work. These were again divided into sections
and subsections by the university authorities. The *Trivium* was
the first stage: hence our adjective *trivial* in the sense of "comparatively unimportant." This comprised Grammar, Rhetoric,
and Logic. Next came the *Quadrivium*, i.e., Arithmetic, Astronomy, Music and Geometry. This was not so great as it sounds;
for the first three were studied only in the most elementary
sense for Church purposes, even where they were seriously
studied at all; and the last, again, only in its most rudimentary
forms. After seven years the student became in England and
France a Master of Arts, in Germany a Doctor of Philosophy:

SOURCE. G. G. Coulton, *Medieval Panorama*, Cambridge, England:
Cambridge University Press, 1938, pp. 411–416. Copyright 1938 by Cambridge
University Press. Reprinted by permission of Cambridge University Press.

different phrases for the same thing. This philosophy was the so-called *scholastic*, a product so definitely medieval that it must be clearly defined before we go farther. It can best be described by noting how far it agrees with or differs from the philosophies of ancient Greece and Rome on the one hand; or on the other, those of modern times. With ancient philosophy it agreed in being based upon dialectics, i.e., upon oral discussion by question and answer; so that even in its most elaborate written forms this dialectic conception is always there, if only in the background. It differed, however, from the ancient in being circumscribed within certain definite theological limits. Modern philosophy, on the other hand, differs from the scholastic on both points. It is not usually dialectic in form; nor again are its foundations circumscribed by authority. This Scholasticism was a natural product of a book-hungry but comparatively bookless age. In the best cathedral schools, teaching had been Socratic. Bishop Fulbert, walking to and fro with his pupils on that cathedral terrace at Chartres where we may still stand and look over the river and the valley, discoursed daily to them upon the deepest questions of life and death; and the two brothers who brought that school to its highest pitch in the first half of the twelfth century, Bernard and Thierry, worked naturally by the same methods.

But the sudden rediscovery of all Aristotle's philosophical writings through translations from the Arabic disturbed the balance of these older schools. The humanists who write towards the close of the twelfth century are full of complaints at the increasing neglect of grammatical and historical training, and the undisciplined rawness of the young philosophers. John of Salisbury and Giraldus Cambrensis complained bitterly on this point; and a century later Roger Bacon spoke out still more plainly, with the exaggeration of personal rivalry. He was a little older than St. Thomas Aquinas, of whom and of other conspicuous university philosophers of his time he writes: "These are boys of the two Student Orders . . . who in many cases enter those Orders at or below the age of twenty years. This is the common course, from the English Sea to the farthest confines of Christendom, and more especially beyond the realm of France; so that in Aquitaine, Provence, Spain, Italy, Germany, Hungary, Denmark, and everywhere, boys are promiscuously received into the

Orders from their tenth to their twentieth year; boys too young to be able to know anything worth knowing, even though they were not already possessed with the aforesaid causes of human error; wherefore, at their entrance into the Orders, they know nought that profiteth to theology." Elsewhere he enters into greater detail, and criticizes the Scholastics of his age in very much the same terms which might have been used by Hume or Thomas Huxley. Their works, he says, are architecturally most imposing, but they rest upon an insecure foundation; upon a Bible misunderstood, an Aristotle misunderstood, and almost total neglect of the mathematical and physical sciences. With regard to Aristotle, Bacon is exaggerated and unjust. It is true that his authority was looked upon as almost sacrosanct, second only to that of the Bible; yet the translations which St. Thomas Aquinas, among others, caused to be made straight from Greek into Latin for his own use are far more correct than Bacon's words would lead us to suppose. With regard to the Bible, however, it is difficult to exaggerate the disadvantage at which Scholasticism stood under the influence of what may fairly be called the bibliolatry of the Middle Ages. This was, in a great measure, inherited from Judaism. To quote from *The Jewish Encyclopaedia:* "The traditional view is that the Pentateuch in its entirety emanated from God, every verse and letter being consequently inspired; hence the tannaitic statement that 'he who says the Torah is not from Heaven is a heretic, a despiser of the Word of God, one who has no share in the world to come.' . . . Moses wrote the whole Pentateuch at God's dictation, even, according to R. Simeon, the last eight verses, relating to his own death." So, again, according to St. Thomas, the primary interpretation of Holy Writ must be the historical or literal. In this sense one word may, indeed, have different significations according to different contexts. But the literal sense is that which the Author intends: and the Author of Holy Writ is God. There can be no falsehood anywhere in the literal sense of Holy Scripture. We must, indeed, make allowance for certain obvious limitations to the theory of plenary inspiration: (1) the limitations of human language, especially at a remote period; (2) limitations imposed by the primitive mentality of the writer's contemporaries; and (3) the fact that figurative or allegorical language lends itself to misinterpretation by hasty or ignorant readers. But he insists that, wherever the *literal* sense conveys a *statement of fact*, that fact must not be questioned. For instance: "Those things which are said of [the Earthly] Paradise in Scripture are put before us by the method of historical narration. But, in all things which Scripture thus hands down, we must hold to the truth of the story as our foundation, and fabricate our spiritual expositions upon that foundation." Thus [he continues] although the Tree of Life is also a spiritual idea (Proverbs iii. 18), yet there is also an actual Tree of Life growing to the present day in the Earthly Paradise—which Aquinas, of course, located as Dante did. Again, in another section of the *Summa*, St. Thomas exemplifies most significantly his view of what might be the literal statement of a passage. Commenting on Exodus xxxiii. 11, "And the Lord spoke to Moses face to face, as a man is wont to speak to his friend," St. Thomas says: "When Scripture states that He [the Lord] spoke to him [Moses], this is to be understood as expressing the opinion of the people who thought that Moses was speaking with God, mouth to mouth." God has not in fact a mouth; that word, taken literally, would be grossly anthropomorphic. But where, for instance, we come across a clear statement of historical fact, that must not be questioned. To deny that Elkanah was Samuel's father would be contrary to the Catholic Faith, "for it follows that the Divine Scripture would be false."

A couple of generations later, William of Ockham dealt with the same point. He had many reasons for differing from St. Thomas, not only as a Franciscan (to whom Dominicans were by that time often rivals and almost enemies), but also because he did not share the standpoint of Aquinas on several important questions. Yet on this question of Biblical inspiration he is, if possible, still more emphatic. He recurs to it over and over again in his *Dialogus*. The Pope himself may not contradict any biblical detail; it would be heresy in a Pope "if, for instance, he were to preach that David was not the son of Jesse, or that Jeroboam had not been King of Israel." In other places he gives similar concrete instances; it would be heretical to deny that Solomon was Bathsheba's son. It was this spirit which made it almost inevitable for the seventeenth-century Roman Congregation, with papal approval, to condemn Galileo as a man who was guilty of having pushed his scientific speculations to a point which brought them into flat contradiction with Bible certainties. We may see this especially in St. Thomas (for it is better still to take him as the crucial example) if we trace two of his most remarkable conclusions back to their source. In one section, after full discussion, he decides definitely that the joy of the Blessed in Heaven will be increased by the sight of the Damned wallowing beneath, in a Hell which he describes (perhaps in virtue of his more voluminous work) at greater length and in cruder terms than Calvin in his *Institutes*. The Blessed will not, of course, rejoice in all these infernal torments *per se,* but incidentally, "considering in them the order of God's justice, and their own liberation, whereat they will rejoice." How can he thus decide, it may be asked, after he himself has pointed out that to rejoice in another's pains may be ordinarily classed as hatred, and that God does not delight in men's pains? Those apparently invincible natural considerations are brushed aside by one plain Bible text: "The just shall rejoice when he shall see the revenge." That vindictive verse of a Hebrew poet, to St. Thomas, outweighs everything else. So was it with Peter Lombard in his *Sentences,* the first permanently standard book of scholastic philosophy: so is it with Thomas's fellow-Dominican and contemporary, the great encyclopaedist Vincent of Beauvais; so is it with St. Bonaventura, in spite of Franciscan humanity; so is it even in early Renaissance times with that other great Franciscan Scholastic and saint, Bernardino of Siena. He, indeed, even outdoes his predecessors and contemporaries, pointing out that all musical harmony needs not only soft but also deep and stern voices, and that God's harmony of heaven could not be complete without these bellowings of the Damned. Not one of these men was sufficiently shocked by his terrible conclusion to look back critically at his premises, and to realize that the logic which had forced him forward to these horrors reposed upon the first fundamental error of bibliolatry, combined with the blind acceptance of an eschatology which owed perhaps almost as much to pagan barbarism as to the Bible.

29 FROM   *Helen Waddell*
                The Wandering Scholars

*In this selection, the gifted historian of medieval literature and
thought Helen Waddell conveys the sense of intellectual adventure
characteristic of the "Twelfth-Century Renaissance."*

Abelard is the first of the new order: the scholar for scholarship's sake. Patrimony and knighthood he left to a younger
brother, recognising in himself a vocation for letters as some
men might for religion: and though he died in such a fashion
that Peter the Venerable writes of it with a sort of heartbroken
passion of reverence, he knew it for the breaking of the proudest
scholar in Europe. It is easy to belittle Abelard's achievement,
the depth and originality of his thinking, the harmony of his
poetry, the quality of his prose. It remains that he is one of the
makers of life, and perhaps the most powerful, in twelfth century
Europe. Paris would have had its university without the magnet
that drew all men thither in the great years when "Rhinoceros
indomitus"[1] lifted up his horn on Mont St. Geneviève and the
schools became a bullring, where opponent after opponent tosses
on the horns of his deadly logic. His tremendous weight flung
into dialectic and philosophy did but incline a balance already
swaying, for north of the Alps, in this as in the other Renaissance,
the current always flows from pure humanism to speculative
theology.

> "*O nightingale, give over*
> *For an hour,*
> *Till the heart sings,*"

would have been written, even if Abelard had not come to

---

[1] The wild rhinoceros.

SOURCE. Helen Waddell, *The Wandering Scholars*, Boston: Houghton
Mifflin Company, 1927, pp. 115–121. Copyright 1927 by Houghton Mifflin.
Reprinted by permission of Barnes and Noble, Inc.

neglect the schools for a windflower of seventeen growing in the shadow of Notre Dame, and set her lovely name to melodies lovelier still. But he stamped himself on the imagination of the century in a fashion beside which Petrarch's influence on the sixteenth becomes the nice conduct of a clouded pane. "Lucifer hath set," said Philippe of Harvengt when he died. "Was there a town or village," cried Heloïse, "but seethed at the word of your coming? What eye but followed you as you went by?" "Sublime in eloquence," wrote a man who hated him. Even Guillaume of Saint Thierry who loosed the storm upon him, said "And yet I loved him." In the schools he kept his sword like a dancer: Goliath they called him with the club of Hercules, another Proteus, flashing from philosophy to poetry, from poetry to wild jesting: a scholar with the wit of a jongleur, and the graces of a *grand seigneur*.[2] His personality, no less than his claim for reason against authority, was an enfranchisement of the human mind. Two things show the efficacy of that dynamic, almost daemonic force, the vibrating fear in the letter of St. Bernard of Clairvaux, *vehementissimus Christi amator*,[3] but a good hater of the brethren—"He hath ascended into heaven: he hath descended into hell": and the last paragraph of the letter in which Peter the Venerable, Abbot of Cluny, broke to Heloïse, now Abbess of the Paraclete, that he who had been hers, *tuo illo*, Master Peter Abelard, was dead. Their love had been a streetsong in Paris: the outrageous vengeance of the girl's uncle on her lover and tardily made husband had been a blazoned scandal; Abelard himself had come to write of it as a surgeon cauterises a wound. Peter the Venerable was an austere man, a stern disciplinarian of his order: but the tragic splendour of it, the marred beauty of these star-crossed lovers whose violent delight had had so violent an end, triumphs over the ecclesiastic's prejudice, and at the last the gracious compassionate prose quickens into a strange, almost lyrical exaltation. He has written of the last days in the great monastery where Abelard, the heretic hounded by two councils, had come to die, "and by so coming enriched us," says its Abbot, with almost a shout of defiance at St. Bernard and his eager pack, "with a wealth beyond all gold." Peter had

[2] Great lord.
[3] Christ's most vehement lover.

done what he could, had forced him to take senior rank; and now stands abashed before the mystery of this man's life whom the love of God and the hate of men had broken, yet left greater in his ruin. Content with the barest, he asked for nothing; Peter, walking behind him in the procession of the relics, *pene stupebam*,[4] all but halted amazed at the bearing of this man who had had the proudest name in France, "humbler than St. Martin, lowlier than St. Germain." Constant at the sacraments, often in prayer: for ever silent, speaking only familiarly with the brethren at meals, or when urged sometimes to speak of divine things in assembly: even to the last, for ever bowed over his books. "Thus Master Peter brought his days to their end: and he who for his supreme mastery of learning was known well-nigh over the whole world and in all places famous, continuing in the discipleship of Him Who said 'Learn of me, for I am meek and lowly in heart,' so to Him passed over, as I must believe. Him therefore, O sister most dear, him to whom once you clung in the union of the flesh and now in that stronger finer bond of the divine affection, with whom and under whom you have long served the Lord, him, I say, in your place or as another you, hath Christ taken to His breast to comfort him, and there shall keep him, till at the coming of the Lord, the voice of the archangel and the trump of God descending, He shall restore him to your heart again."

Abelard died in 1142: his stormy life is bounded by what is perhaps the greatest half-century of the Middle Ages. The thirteenth century is the full harvesting, the richer in accomplishment, yet the Paris of St. Thomas Aquinas and Saint Bonaventura has lost something of the first madness,

> "*The divine intoxication*
> *Of the first league out from land.*"

That first league, that first half of the twelfth century: Abelard lecturing in Paris; Peter the Venerable travelling in Spain and commissioning a translation of the Koran: Adelard of Bath in Syria and Cilicia, writing his book on natural philosophy and dedicating it to the Bishop of Syracuse; Hermann of Dalmatia translating the *Planisphere* of Ptolemy and dedicating it to

[4] Almost stunned.

Thierry of Chartres, "the soul of Plato reincarnate, firm anchor in the tempest-tossed flux of our studies": Thierry lecturing on the new Aristotle, just restored to scholarship: Paris for the first time become the *patria* of the mind, the rival in men's hearts of Rome. By the thirteenth century she has a University with statutes and privileges and set books and courses that prescribe Priscian *magnum et minorem*, and then alas! omit the classics altogether. But in the glorious liberty of the children of Paris of the twelfth, the scholars come up, young and old, and demand the point and the line, the nature of universals, of Fate and Free Will, the sources of the Nile, dividing in the taverns the undivided Trinity, and one calls to the other to abandon this for that. Literature was to make a man's fortune. Had not Maurice de Sully come to Paris begging his bread, and now behold him its Bishop? And Nicholas Breakspear, the shabby Englishman, the "spoiled monk" of St. Albans, sheltering under St. Denys, picking up what crumbs of learning he could; behold him Bishop of Albano, Cardinal Legate, Lord Pope himself. Petrus Pictor had in vain prophesied

> "*How to be a beggar and a fool? Would you know it?*
> *Let you read books and learn to be a poet.*"

had in vain seen Ignorance go by in full pontificals, on a good horse, clean and splendid and well washed in warm water, and Aristotle barefoot on the road, the dust on his feet and his stick, a few books of grammar in his knapsack. Their disillusionment was to fill Europe with disgruntled scholars who could not dig, but to beg were not ashamed, who died under the ban of the Church, and made great verse and grievous scandal. But that is still to come. Men do not yet know which is *utile* among the arts, but write hopefully home that "as Cato said, to know anything is praiseworthy," and they live in a garret, with one gown for lectures among them, and play at dice with the neighbour's cat for a fourth. The whole brief sweetness of it in the opening sentence of a story told by an unknown Irish scholar: "In those first days when youth in me was happy and life was swift in doing, and I wandering in the divers cities of sweet France, for the desire that I had of learning, gave all my might to letters." John of Salisbury writes of Paris with the subdued warmth, the

steady heat of his affection transfiguring his sober prose. Guido de
Bazoches becomes sheerly lyrical: "Paris, queen among cities, moon
among stars, so gracious a valley [as it is to this day from the
terraces of St. Germain], an island of royal palaces. . . . And
on that island hath Philosophy her royal and ancient seat: who
alone, with Study her sole comrade, holding the eternal citadel
of light and immortality, hath set her victorious foot on the
withering flower of the fast ageing world."

CONCLUSION

The preceding pages have documented briefly, first, the historical debate over the question of a "Twelfth-Century Renaissance" and, second, some of the important forces of change at work in twelfth-century Western Europe: the rise of towns and commerce, the growth of constitutionalism in political institutions and theory, the flowering of twelfth-century humanism and rationalism, literature and love, and the momentous artistic shift from Romanesque to Gothic. Did these changes constitute a renaissance? The reader must arrive at his own answer.

But "must" is perhaps too strong a word. For the answer to the renaissance question is immeasurably less important than an understanding of the changes themselves. It was recently said of an obscure developing nation in the Middle East that this country had, through economic aid, leapt in a single decade all the way from the eleventh century—into the twelfth! The remark was good wit but bad history, relying as it did on a discredited stereotype of the dark and changeless Middle Ages. In truth, the leap of the twelfth century was one of the greatest that Europe has made. Perhaps it was, as C. H. McIlwain suggested, a greater leap than that of the Italian Renaissance.

And perhaps not. A thorough study of the twelfth century leaves us as ignorant of Renaissance Italy as was Burckhardt of the High Middle Ages. Important things were occurring in twelfth-century Europe; other, very different things were occurring in Renaissance Italy. Both ages were singularly vital. Both were crucial epochs of transformation and transition. And both demand critical, sympathetic study—of what they were, in and of themselves, and what they contributed to the development and enrichment of civilization.

BIBLIOGRAPHICAL ESSAY

I. THE HASKINS THESIS. Most of the passages in this book are excerpts from longer works, and the student who wishes to pursue the problem further should read those works in full. C. H. Haskins, *The Renaissance of the Twelfth Century* (Meridian Paperback) is, of course, the basic text. Important commentary on the Haskins thesis will be found in the following articles: Erwin Panofsky, "Renaissance and Renascences," *Kenyon Review*, VI (1944), 201-36; Urban T. Holmes, "The Idea of a Twelfth-Century Renaissance," *Speculum*, XXVI (1951), 643-51; R. W. Southern, "The Place of England in the Twelfth-Century Renaissance," *History*, XLV (1960), 201-16; W. A. Nitze, "The So-Called Twelfth-Century Renaissance," *Speculum*, XXIII (1948), 464-71; and the article by E. M. Sanford printed in full (but without the authors' footnotes) in this volume. For students who read French, *La renaissance du xiie siècle: Les écoles et l'enseignement*, by G. Paré, A. Brunet, and P. Tremblay (Paris, Ottawa, 1933), will be valuable. From the viewpoint of the Italian Renaissance the problem can be best approached through W. K. Ferguson, *The Renaissance in Historical Thought* (Boston, 1948).

II. WHAT HAPPENED IN THE TWELFTH CENTURY? Here the bibliography is virtually infinite, and only a sampling of works can be suggested. Probably the best general book on the period is R. W. Southern, *The Making of the Middle Ages* (Yale Paperback). Many sections in Marc Bloch's masterful *Feudal Society* (2 vols., Phoenix Paperback) are relevant to the question. Frederick Heer's *The Medieval World* (Mentor Paperback) presents an interesting contrast between the dynamism of the twelfth century and the stabilization of the subsequent period. *Twelfth-Century Europe and the Foundations of Modern Society*, edited by Marshall Clagett, Gaines Post, and Robert Reynolds (Madison, Wisc., 1961), contains a number of excellent short articles on various aspects of twelfth-

166 Bibliographical Essay

century civilization. The social history of the period is illuminated in Urban T. Holmes, *Daily Living in the Twelfth Century* (Wisconsin Paperbacks), based on the observations of the twelfth-century traveler and scholar Alexander Neckam. For a gloomier picture see Achille Luchaire, *Social France in the Age of Philip Augustus* (Harper Paperback), and the various writings of G. G. Coulton—for example, *Medieval Panorama* (Meridian Paperback).

On economic change it is best to start with the works of Henri Pirenne: *Medieval Cities* (Anchor Paperback), and *The Economic and Social History of Medieval Europe* (Harvest Paperback). On political institutions see Robert Fawtier, *The Capetian Kings of France* (St. Martin's Paperback); A. L. Poole, *From Domesday Book to Magna Carta* (2nd ed., Oxford, 1955); and Geoffrey Barraclough, *Medieval Germany* (2 vols., Oxford, 1938). The standard one-volume account of political theory is C. H. McIlwain, *The Growth of Political Thought in the West* (New York, 1932). For a more recent analysis, see Walter Ullmann, *A History of Political Thought: The Middle Ages* (Penguin Paperback). John of Salisbury's *Statesman's Book* (selections from the *Policraticus*) has been translated by John Dickinson (New York, 1927). For a view of John of Salisbury as a literary scholar see H. Liebeschutz, *Medieval Humanism in the Life and Writings of John of Salisbury* (London, 1950). Medieval humanism, courtly love, and rationalism are all treated thoughtfully and gracefully by H. O. Taylor, *The Medieval Mind* (4th ed., 2 vols., Cambridge, Mass., 1951).

C. S. Lewis, *The Allegory of Love* (Oxford Galaxy Paperback) is an excellent introduction to the literature of medieval romantic love. The subject is treated deftly and wittily by Sidney Painter, "Feudalism and Western Civilization," in *Feudalism and Liberty*, edited by F. A. Cazel (Baltimore, 1961). For sensitive translations of the lyric poetry of the period see Helen Waddell, *Medieval Latin Lyrics* (Penguin Paperback). On Abelard and Héloïse see the splendid chapter, "The Heart of Héloïse," in Taylor's *Medieval Mind* (cited above); Etienne Gilson, *Héloïse and Abélard* (Chicago, 1951); and Helen Waddell's fine historical novel, *Peter Abelard* (Compass Paperback). Abelard's *Story of My Misfortunes* has been translated by H. A. Bellows (Glencoe, Ill., 1958).

The subjects of Romanesque and Gothic art are well covered in Henri Focillon, *The Art of the West in the Middle Ages* (2 vols.,

London, 1963), and Whitney S. Stoddard, *Monastery and Cathedral in France* (Middletown, Conn., 1966). On the Gothic style more particularly, see O. G. von Simson, *The Gothic Cathedral* (London, 1956); J. F. Fitchen, *The Construction of Gothic Cathedrals* (New York, 1961); and Erwin Panofsky, *Gothic Architecture and Scholasticism* (Meridian Paperback), which bridges medieval architecture and medieval rationalism.

There are numerous surveys of medieval thought, all of which discuss high-medieval rationalism (or scholasticism). Dom David Knowles' *The Evolution of Medieval Thought* (Vintage Paperback) is relatively light and brief. For a detailed study in one volume see Etienne Gilson, *The History of Christian Philosophy in the Middle Ages* (New York, 1955). The medieval scientific achievement is presented with sympathy and erudition in A. C. Crombie, *Medieval and Early Modern Science* (2 vols., Anchor Paperback). On the medieval universities see C. H. Haskins, *The Rise of the Universities* (Cornell Paperback), and—much more detailed—Hastings Rashdall, *The Universities of Europe in the Middle Ages* (new ed., 3 vols., Oxford, 1936).